Echo Selling

How to Reach a New Generation of Buyers Through Their Influencers

Steve Bookbinder

Braughler™
Books
braughlerbooks.com

Printed in the United States of America
Published by Braughler Books LLC., Springboro, Ohio

First printing, 2022

ISBN: 978-1-955791-19-9

Library of Congress Control Number: 2021921834

Ordering information: Special discounts are available on quantity purchases by bookstores, corporations, associations, and others. For details, contact the publisher at:

sales@braughlerbooks.com

or at 937-58-BOOKS

For questions or comments about this book, please write to:

info@braughlerbooks.com

Braughler™
Books
braughlerbooks.com

Dedication

This book is dedicated to the sales professionals I have met who have inspired me—the ones who view sales as a sport and are constantly looking for three things: to give themselves a professional edge, to share their best ideas with others and to have fun along the way.

I am especially grateful to Fran Proto, my wife and editor, whose attention to detail brings quality control to a new level. Her ability to find a creative solution to the problems I encountered while writing this book—as well as the other problems in my life—is the secret to any success I have experienced.

I would like to thank Molly Protosow, who has been indispensable during the more than ten years we have worked together. Without her ongoing help and support, this book project would never have gotten past the "thinking about it" stage.

Thanks also to Bill Acker, who has coached me in sales and training, provided valuable insights and helped me to shape the content of this book once I got past writing the title.

David Moore, who apart from being a role model to myself and countless other business professionals, has been my friend, business partner and English Channel swim team captain. Without him, I would not have had many of the adventures I experienced along the way. I am forever grateful and can't thank him enough.

Finally, I would like to acknowledge David Braughler and his team for the guidance and encouragement I received throughout the writing process.

Contents

Introduction

Echo Selling emerged from my observation that salespeople in every industry talk about something that never made any sense to me: finding the one *right* person also known as the buyer or decision maker.

Every salesperson talks about Qualifying but despite their efforts, they end up talking to the wrong person. No matter how many different ways the seller asks who the decision maker is during the qualifying phase ("Are you the decision maker? Are you sure?), the customer changes their original answer the moment the salesperson hands them their proposal ("now I'll have to talk to my boss, the committee, my team").

Given that I also sell – in my case I sell sales training – I see firsthand that there is never a single decision maker.

Even the owner of a tiny company always shares their next decision with their team before they finalize their decision. The team is sometimes their assistant, their employees, their business partners, their spouse or family members. What I learned from talking to my customers is that sometimes the buyer brought up the idea of buying something new to their team – just to hear their reaction. Sometimes the idea came from the team. But, most often, it came from somebody other than the salesperson. The customer was at an industry event or read an article or watched an interview or read a book which got them thinking…and the next thing you know, they called someone and talked. Somehow, the idea snowballed into a call to me or some other vendor they ended up buying from.

Like a witness to a car accident who is unable to recall the exact details of the blur of the scene they just saw, the buyer can never quite recall precisely how someone else's idea became their own. Or how they went from not sure to very sure when making a purchase decision. Or how a total stranger suddenly became an influential thought leader in their head. But that mysterious process seemed to be behind virtually every sale that I worked on and my clients reported to me.

As I explored the idea, I became consumed by the psychology behind decision making, influencing and messaging.

The more I thought about it, the more I realized for a sale to close, someone has to make a decision. The problem is no one likes making decisions and most never make one until their back is against the wall. The most common decision people make is the decision to delay making a decision. Why? Because there is too much risk in "owning a decision" especially for the Business-to-Business buyer. For that reason, the "buying conversation" isn't between the seller and the customer. It is later when the buyer is talking to their circle of influencers who reassure each other until they feel safe about making a decision.

When you explore every sale, as I have, especially the failed sales that include a long delay, you realize how important this principle is to sales success. How do we get someone to make a decision? Talk them into it? No! That only leads to ineffective sales habits. The best way is for the customer to talk themselves into buying decisions. How? Leverage the existing echo chamber where buyers and influencers live until they echo the seller's pitch.

Echo Selling explains how this principle has always been the unspoken force behind buying decisions. And it provides the strategies and tactics salespeople need to use to build a sales strategy that will bring them more sales and lead to a more successful sales career.

PART 1

Understanding Echo Selling

What is Echo Selling?
Echo selling is when the salesperson gets their customer to repeat the seller's words to the customer's circle of influencers.

First, let's clarify words we thought we already understood
Echo is the voice that amplifies your own voice.

Selling isn't another word for persuading. It's a system of activities for finding ever more efficient ways to create lead flow and deal flow.

Echo Selling is the way to get your voice to amplify to others so you can efficiently reach more people and close more sales.

You already know Echo Selling; you just didn't have a name for it
Decisions have always been made the same way: when two parties talk together. Those two parties are the "decision maker(s)" and their circle of influencers, who include their partner, team, peers, and/or boss. Salespeople are not in those conversations. But when we get our sales pitch into those conversations, both parties influence each other to buy from us.

Echo Selling leverages this natural communication between decision makers and their circle of influencers by encouraging them to echo the seller's pitch to each other.

> *The Takeaway: This book explains how Echo Selling reaches decision makers and those who influence them.*

Sell the way people buy
Echo Selling is not a new "how-to" sales program. The promise of

each new sales system is that it works. Well, they all work some of the time. Sometimes you get the sale whether or not you are consultative, challenging or spinning.

What really matters is how customers buy.

Do you know how and why your customers buy? Most salespeople don't. We tend to study our losses but not our wins. The real story behind why someone buys almost always involves someone else — the boss, the team, the coworkers, the peers or trusted thought leader — providing reassurance to the decision maker. When the customer buys, there was an echo during the exchange between the customer and the other person or people. That echo is the sound of a salesperson's words about the urgency of the customer's problem and the relevance of that salesperson's solution. When you don't get a sale, the echo wasn't there.

To understand, let's look at why customers don't buy … The number one reason is "lack of reassurance." Number two is "fear of change." In both cases, the customer never received the "safety" net of reassurance from the people they trust.

Echo Selling happens when the customer receives the reassurance they need from their co-workers, peers, team and boss.

I always knew that people buy with their emotions and later rationalize their decision. Echo Selling is proof! It works because of the emotional element of buying.

> **The Takeaway: Echo Selling explains why customers buy.**

Who is Steve Bookbinder?

My job is to learn what the best salespeople are doing, test the best ideas personally and summarize my findings in my newest workshops and videos. I have trained, coached, managed and mentored more than 50,000 salespeople, managers and owners. I've delivered more than 5,000 in-person workshops and more than 500 SKOs (sales kickoffs). In 2020, I conducted more than 100 virtual workshops, webinars and SKOs to sales teams throughout Asia/Pacific (APAC), Europe/Middle East/Africa (EMEA), North and South America. Why do I tell you that? Because I want you to know I have talked to — and continue to learn from — a lot of great salespeople and managers all over the world.

What I have learned is that Echo Selling is a missed opportunity. Sellers around the world are missing their goals. Is the answer for them to keep doing what they are doing but work even harder? No.

Hard work alone doesn't solve the problem that customers are harder to reach than ever. Today's customers are armed to the teeth with technology designed to block salespeople. Today's salespeople need new skills to keep up with their moving target. Echo Selling is the new skill everyone, from experienced sales pros to new-hires, need to adopt and adapt in order to reach and engage more customers. Echo Selling gets your sales pitch to people you can never directly meet regardless of how hard you work.

> **The Takeaway: I have talked to thousands of salespeople all over the world. I've saved you the trouble of traveling 4 million air miles, spending 4,000 nights in hotels and spending countless hours in Zoom meetings to learn the best sales practices. You don't have to thank me, but you should go into Echo Selling with an open mind.**

Sales is about paying your bills every month, not merely closing one sale

The reality of the sales job is that the goals, expectations and challenges change every year. For this reason, if you keep selling the same way every year, even if you are "doing everything right," you will have inconsistent results. That is why conventional sales training, where some *expert* teaches you the steps of the sale, seems unnecessary to so many salespeople.

People in sales for many years have learned that sales is unique among careers in that the goals go up every year. Reaching those ever-rising goals is often the difference between paying your monthly bills and being able to afford new ones. My sales training addresses this real-world challenge, which all sales teams face. My expertise isn't merely knowing how to sell. It is in solving the real-world problem of adapting to ever-changing market conditions and hitting ever-harder-to-reach goals in order to have a successful sales career.

My sales training begins with extensive due diligence with each client. By direct observation of salespeople and their pipelines (and forecasting accuracy), I have learned what sales techniques, strategies and habits pay off and which ones no longer work because of business changes and technology developments.

Before I introduce a new skill, I test it myself. If the technique works for me, too, it becomes part of my training skill set. Echo Selling is my newest technique.

> **The Takeaway: Even if you know how to sell, you need to keep training yourself how to have a successful sales career. Echo Selling puts you – and keeps you - on the path to a successful career.**

Nothing motivates a salesperson better than finding an easier way

Let's consider this question: What's one thing you always have time for even when you are working so hard there is no time for anything else? The answer is the easy sale.

I have a burning interest in learning a better, faster, more efficient way to sell. My clients want that advice and I want it for my own sales. I am on a lifelong journey to find the best ideas that will help us all overcome our sales challenges.

My newest discovery is that for all of us to make more sales, we need for some of those sales to be easier to close. Echo Selling produces "easy sales."

What's the easiest sale? Sales with very short sales cycles. There are two kinds of easy sales. The first is an inbound lead which "easily" converts into a sale with the fewest number of conversations. The second is a big sale that closes quickly, even though there are a lot of influencers. Echo Selling is perfect for both.

> ***The Takeaway: I was looking for more easy sales when I discovered Echo Selling.***

You don't get paid more – or more often – for hard sales

Nobody ever tells you about the Easy Sale. Instead, we like to talk about the hard-to-get sale, many of which are great "sales adventure stories." You can use those stories your entire career and even after you retire. Someday, you'll repeat the story to anyone you are trying to impress.

The easy sale is the under-appreciated sale. No one respects the brilliance of the easy sale. So, no one talks about them, even though they produce the most scalable business model with the lowest cost-per-sale.

If you are in business long enough, you will occasionally get an easy sale. When I first got my own, I realized I wanted more of those. I've been on a mission ever since for both kinds of easy sales: inbound leads that convert as well as easier-to close-big sales.

In my quest for easy sales, I learned there is a gap between what most salespeople tell their customer and what that customer hears and tells their circle of influencers. I discovered Echo Selling closes that gap. Echo Selling works by getting the customer to "optimally" echo the salesperson's pitch to the right influencers in just the right way. Sales pitches echo best when they are easily repeatable, position the problem as urgent and the solution relevant —with an important difference versus competitive offerings.

Ironically, Echo Selling can help you produce easy sales — and it's simple — but it's not easy. It's not one thing you do on social media. It's not one thing you add to your emails. It's not one page you add to your presentation. One thing I have learned about life in general, and Echo Selling in particular, is that the last step always looks easy. Like an inbound lead just when you need one. Often easy things look like luck. However, the steps that began that journey were not luck. If you follow all the right principles that I have arranged into this playbook, you can personalize your path to more easy sales.

> *The Takeaway: Sales are easier when your sales pitch echoes to the people you can't reach. It's worth the hard work of Echo Selling to get more Easy Sales.*

Where Echo Selling fits into the buying process:
When salespeople, especially salespeople who've had a lot of training, discuss the customer's buying journey, they usually simplify it into about 3 steps — Qualify, Present & Close. Some describe 4 or 5 steps. The actual number of steps that buyers can take is much longer. For example, digital marketing data experts can point to car buyers completing 300-500 online steps before they test drive a car. And, then they have a few more steps immediately afterwards. Consumers complete cycles of research often beginning with social media and Google results pages which lead to repeat visits to brand websites, competitor's sites and eventually review sites. Maybe a few YouTube videos and "expert opinion" blogs/articles/newsletters/podcasts along the way, too, just to be sure. The business buyer has become more like the consumer, preferring to spend the first 50-75% of their buying journey looking into something before even talking to a salesperson.

Why does it take so many steps? Here are a few reasons:

- Confusion over budget authority and budget decision process — your contact wants to buy but isn't sure how to navigate those waters because they are new to their company or role.

- Buying something to solve a new problem brings the opportunity to look very good or very bad. In the same way people want to kill the messenger, when a person brings into their company the wrong new solution provider, they are at risk if the solution doesn't work (or doesn't work as well as others thought it would). They believe it may be safer to delay, stall, wait whenever possible.

- Politically, you cover yourself if your decisions follow a rigorous process with lots of input from all the right people.

- To salespeople who are usually in a rush to finally close the deal, it feels like customers move like glaciers even when they tell you they are hurrying things along. Meanwhile, the customer thinks they are moving fast when they:

- Recognize and discuss a problem during a meeting
- Study the problem within a few weeks
- Spend the next few weeks / months gathering input
- Wait for the right moment to share findings
- Spend as long as needed to campaign where needed to gather all of the political support and necessary approvals
- Even after everyone hinted approval, the buyer may need another few weeks doing a *final check* to make sure everyone is truly on board with the decision

Then, of course, there is procurement and legal. Then we have to wait for kickoff meetings to get scheduled. No wonder salespeople are so anxious. Most of the time, their sale is in danger. At every step, the buyer can abandon the process. And they will if anyone along the way makes a funny face when offering their opinion about a suggested solution. So much is riding on reading the facial expressions of people who influence the buyer. ⌃ = no sale; ⌃⌃ = sale!

> **The Takeaway: It's the salesperson's job to put a smile on influencer's faces when buyers talk to them about your sale. Echo selling is the best way to influence those reactions.**

Echo Selling solves the biggest problem: your pipeline

How you sell determines your output.

Most of my clients tell me their main goal is *more sales* followed closely by *more qualified prospects*. Better sales pipelines solve both of those problems. Why? Because sales come from pipelines.

I've reviewed thousands of pipelines and heard many sales stories. Many remind me of stories I used to tell my boss, especially the ones that begin with " … well, this one is different … ."

The one thing that would improve most people's pipelines is having more opportunities that are advancing to the next step within their normal sales cycle. Echo Selling inspires the customer to agree to - or even reach out to suggest — next steps soon.

> **The Takeaway: Echo Selling improves the health of your pipeline. Lack of Echo Selling is the root cause of unhealthy pipelines.**

Buyers echo before they buy

The foundation ideas of Echo Selling have been evolving for years. It all began for me years ago, when I was a struggling salesperson at my first sales training company trying to find new clients. Usually, larger, more famous training companies would win if the sale went to an RFP (Request for Proposal or Tender Offer). As a competitive person, I was determined to beat those competitors, especially the ones that were more well known.

Whenever I am trying to improve anything, I begin by tracking my current conversion rate and then change one thing. The thing I changed was to get to "influencers" *before* the company went to RFP and enhance my pitch with "sound bites" (unique terms, phrases and metaphors) about my training. My conversion rate dramatically improved! You might argue that the early meeting gave me a relationship head-start when the sale finally went to RFP. While that is probably true, the biggest clue I had was something more obvious: when the RFP included some of my sound bites, I beat my competition for the training engagement. For my words to survive long enough to get into the final draft of the RFP, the co-workers who wrote the RFP must have reacted positively to my sound bites.

What I learned by optimizing my RFP process was that my pitch, when successfully echoed, got the customer and their circle to think my idea was actually their idea first. After I gave them a word to describe the problems my solutions addressed, they suddenly realized they had that problem, too, and needed a solution.

> ***The Takeaway: Echo Selling can improve your conversion rates. When salespeople strategically create easily repeatable sound bites, customers will choose to use those sound bites when talking to their circle of influencers. Echo Selling reaches people that can't be reached through conventional selling and prospecting.***

The curious psychology of Echo Selling

My next discovery about the power of Echo Selling came when I was looking for an efficient way to get existing customers to buy my new training programs. My challenge was — and still is — that most of my time and 100% of my interest - is in helping salespeople. I would prefer to sell services that my clients ask for, from a customer service point of view. But, from a scalable business strategy perspective, I need to deliver services that are not only valuable but repeatable. How can I get customers to ask me about new programs that I would like to offer them? Before I had a name for it, I used Echo Selling to sell my clients my new programs.

For my idea to work, I needed the actual decision maker to be in the room during a workshop I was conducting for their company. Even though that decision maker was trying to be a *fly on the wall* in the back of the room, I played to them, without looking directly at them, even while answering participant's questions. When the question was about some content outside of the scope of that day's workshop, I answered by saying "let me see if I can help you … .if we had more time, I'd get into XYZ (my new program), which solves the sales challenge you just asked about … .." The more descriptive the title of the other program, the more often the decision maker heard it, remembered it and came up to me during the next break to ask me about that program they "overheard" me mention in class ("...hey, I was thinking, we need help with *our* XYZ skills. Can you tell me about your XYZ training?")

> ***The Takeaway: The power of overhearing something can be stronger than the power of an overt sales pitch.***

Echo Selling Worked <u>on</u> Me Before It Worked <u>for</u> Me

As a kid, I played the telephone game, which is a seemingly simple game that always produced the same surprising result. The first person would whisper something to the second person who would whisper what they heard to the third person and on and on. The final person would have to say out loud what they heard. And the first person would say what they began with. Guess what? The message was very changed. In fact, upon analysis, we learned that the message began changing when the second person told the third person.

With that game in mind, I realized for Echo Selling to work the sales message had to be easily repeatable. I began looking at easily repeatable expressions beginning with expressions that I was repeating.

For example, several years ago, a client introduced to me the term "second-level question." I'd never heard that expression. I figured that this must be a new business expression which somehow I had missed when it first came out. The imagery suggested by *second-level question* is clear: it sounds like an advanced questioning technique. I was taken with this expression and concerned that I had fallen behind the curve by not knowing about this important new skill. I got to work trying to figure out second-level questions. After much thought, I began mentioning this skill in sales meetings. Eventually, I wrote articles about it.

When these articles started getting attention, I developed a workshop to practice the art and science of using the right second-level question instead of "the usual" question salespeople ask in familiar sales moments.

A few years ago, I made a trip around the world to deliver my second-level question training to a global client. Since then, other clients have requested this training. One client asks for me to repeat this workshop every year.

In my sales process, I'd give prospects this example of a second-level question:

Following a first meeting, if the customer says to the salesperson that they are going to talk to their boss or their team or the committee, most sellers ask "can I come with you?" But they would get more benefit and set themselves up for an informed strategy if they instead asked "will you be recommending us to your boss/team/committee?"

This example almost always gets the prospects to say: *"Our people need to ask second-level questions!"*

Before I used that term, they never thought about the kind of questions their salespeople were asking. But, after hearing the term, my prospects (sales leaders for their organization) knew it was a real problem they needed to address.

It was only after delivering this training to hundreds of salespeople at dozens of companies that I learned that the customer who originally introduced me to this term had in fact made it up. There was no second-level question. He got me to echo his term and I got others to follow suit.

> **The Takeaway: the combination of context, timing and word choice makes Echo Selling work even when the game of telephone does not.**

Echo Selling amplifies in-bound leads and referrals

Have you ever called the shot when playing pool by accurately predicting the outcome of an obviously difficult shot? That's what Echo Selling feels like when you use it in sales. A salesperson with the right level of confidence can call a lead. A highly skilled sale professional can eventually get into a conversation with that person. The best of them can handle the inevitable early objections and hard questions. But can even that person get the lead to call them? I did — and you can too with Echo Selling.

There are a lot of new things in sales jobs, often technology-related, that we are expected to be experts in the day we are introduced to them. Echo Selling is one of those things. Up until now, you never heard of this skill. Going forward, you are going to need it. Your ability to get a sales job will be in part based on it. Your manager will expect you to at least try to Echo Sell. Wait, you're thinking. Won't my new company simply give me inbound leads? Here's a little secret no one tells you: there are never enough inbound leads that are hot enough to close easily. Lead nurturing, handled by the salesperson and marketing department, might warm up some leads. But Echo Selling will heat up those leads quickly, by creating new and unexpected interactions--like popcorn in a microwave.

Sales is a great job, but it's changing. The "old approach," which is any approach that began before March 2020, worked great in a world that doesn't exist anymore. In this new world, B2B (Business to Business) customers increasingly buy like consumers. They go online to search engines and social media. They ask the people they trust for referrals. Meanwhile, more salespeople than ever are reaching out more times than ever in more ways than ever. These customers are getting more messages via email, InMail, SMS, etc. than ever before. Meanwhile they aren't even speaking to salespeople until they are midway or more through their buying process. What's your customer talking about during that first half of their buying process? They're talking about the priority and urgency of their problems as well as their timetable and budget for solutions. Who are they talking to in the first half of their buying journey? They'll say they are having internal discussions. We call internal discussions Echo Buying.

> **The Takeaway: During the first half of the process, the buyer is influenced by their circle of influencers. That is the best time to Echo Sell to that customer.**

I know; your sale is different

Many salespeople believe their sale "*is different.*" They don't see how anyone's advice is going to apply to them. They are sure their customers don't buy differently than the salesperson sells. These sellers believe if they have been selling the same way for decades, then their customers have been buying the same way for decades. But in today's world, even the most unsophisticated customer can do their own research with the click of a button. They're no longer dependent on the salesperson for information about possible solutions to their problems.

I ask those people what they know about sales in different industries and marketplaces around the world. The things about your sale you think are different are in fact just like someone else's sale that you never met — but I have. In some cases, I have multiple clients trying to sell services to the same industry, sometimes the same customer. Each uses a different sales process. Each is sure theirs is the only way that works.

> *The Takeaway: Echo Selling works in your "unique" business, even if you haven't been using it. Echo Selling is how your customers buy.*

The world has changed, have you?

In my workshops over the last few years, I like to remind people how recently we all adopted smart phones and social media. We all have developed online workflows every time we want to know, go, watch or buy. As consumers, we have learned how to buy online. B2B buyers are increasingly shopping like consumers.

There is not one thing we do today the same as we did five years ago. To reach the right people the right number of times with the right message requires many new skills and technologies. We all need to be great at Personal Marketing (combining Email Marketing, Social Selling, phone, text and networking in the right order and with the right cadence on each platform). We need apps that didn't exist a few years ago in order to build our list, customize our email templates, automate messages, test other messages, track new metrics, build our pipeline and optimize our results. We need to re-imagine how to combine classic selling skills like phone prospecting and networking with inbound marketing and ABS (Account Based Selling) programs.

This argues for adopting and adapting. That is, bending and shaping classic skills, like presenting, to influence people who are working from home and living in the digital world.

> *The Takeaway: Not sure about adding Echo Selling to your skill set? If you are still relying on the same techniques that you were using more than five years*

ago it may be time to update your act. The ability to adapt and adopt every year has become the most sought-after selling skill – and the best way to be assured of a brilliant future in the sales profession. Make sure you mention Echo Selling in your job interview if you want them to take you seriously.

When Echo Selling became a reality for me

The best sales strategies begin with the right questions. My favorite question, which has led me to many actionable ideas is who already has a relationship with the people I am trying to sell to? That question led to a strategy which led to me writing this book.

I considered that question as I thought about a lead I wanted to contact. I don't mean "lead" in the modern sense, which is someone who expressed at least a little interest by virtue of their visiting my website. I mean it in the old-fashioned sense: a name on a piece of paper.

I asked myself—who do they know? Who do they talk to? Who talks to them? When do they talk? What is the context of that conversation?

My lead was a "head of sales." As described in the Wizard of Oz who said at the end of the movie that he was going to "hob nob with his fellow wizards," I imagined my lead attending regular meetings with their *fellow wizards*. They would be peers who are the heads of the Account Management, Enterprise, SMB (small and medium-sized businesses), Inside and Business Development teams. Of course, they would also have meetings with their own team, too, specifically their direct report sales managers. And, no doubt, they would be attending Operations Meetings with heads of other departments, like Marketing, Finance and Production.

It occurred to me that any idea I could get to my lead, if taken seriously enough, would enter into the conversations in those meetings. I could visualize those meetings. Let's say I got an email to my lead which they found interesting because it was relevant to the sales challenges that are discussed in their weekly meetings. Best case: they'd bring it up during one of those meetings. Then, they'd look at everyone's face for a reaction (I was assuming a Zoom meeting with everyone's camera on). In that case, I'd need those heads to nod when they heard my lead summarize my email. How good is my lead at summarizing emails? What will it take to get those faces to smile?

With those questions and the goal of getting those people to agree, as a starting point I reached out to my lead. Four weeks later, that lead sent me an email requesting a conversation.

This book describes how I filled those four weeks.

PART 2

Change Your Thinking Before You Can Change Others

Salesperson Thinking vs Digital Thinking

If you are thinking "ok, tell me the magic words that echo," I will tell you that you are not thinking about this correctly. You are still thinking like a salesperson.

If you think Echo Selling is something you simply tack on to your current strategy, you will not experience success. I want you to be successful. I promised you easy sales for a reason: I understand how salespeople think. I want you to know the payoff — get sales, particularly easy sales, that you wouldn't have gotten any other way. I also warned you that getting easy sales isn't easy.

The hard part is transitioning the way you think. Salespeople usually think of *convincing*. For that reason, sellers feel comfortable using as many words as are needed to convince. Sellers hear objections and counterpunch with turnarounds. You know who specializes in thinking like customers? Marketers. Especially digital marketers. Marketers think of persuading by conveying, not convincing. Digital marketers think about targeting the right person with the right message at the right time on the right device in order to get the right ROI (return on investment).

I call the thinking that Echo Sellers need to adopt "digital thinking." You are thinking digitally when you are thinking three-dimensionally:

First dimension ("BEFORE") - You are considering the customer's mindset before you deliver your words — that is, what they are ready to listen to given what they are currently looking to learn.

<u>Second dimension ("DURING")</u> - You are considering the context your words will be viewed in — that is, your words plus all of the messaging the customer is getting from all of their influencers.

<u>Third dimension ("AFTER")</u> - The impact of your words - that is, the customer's actions and future conversations after the sales conversation.

> *The Takeaway: Sellers need to change from "thinking like a salesperson" (convincing others and turning around their objections) to Digital Thinking, which is communicating in a way that produces the desired reaction. To get those right reactions, we need to consider not only the words, but the context, timing, communication platform we use and the range of after-effect actions our words will cause.*

When the student is ready, the teacher will emerge.
People often ask me for recommendations of sales books. I find the most helpful sales books are not about sales. I also learn a lot from movies. The key to gaining the most from each book and movie is your being open and ready to learn, especially about the topics you thought you already knew or thought were irrelevant.

Begin by improving your understanding of:

- Emotional intelligence, which is the ability to see yourself through other's eyes

- Game theory, which considers all possible outcomes — and strategic advantage of each solution - when studying a problem.

- Psychology, so you can better understand why we (salespeople and customers) are motivated to do the things we do.

- Office Politics, which explains how Emotional Intelligence, Game Theory and Psychology combine to cause us to do (and say) the things we do at work. (We'll take a closer look at all of these in parts 3 & 4 of this book).

I recommend you read as much as you can about all of these topics. You can also learn from watching movies to improve your understanding of the "plot lines" or actions that characters take as a reaction to the words and actions of other characters who attempt to influence them.

While there are many movies that you can learn from, Echo Sellers can gain a lot of insight from watching Mission Impossible movies, which tell the story of how to correctly anticipate the psychology and motivation of the person you are targeting. In those movies, the plan is always to get their target to trap themselves. They create illusions but the biggest one is getting the person they are targeting to believe they are choosing their own destiny when they choose to do the very thing our heroes want them to do.

> **The Takeaway: Read books and watch movies with the mindset of what you can learn from each about human nature.**

Just Because You Said Something Doesn't Mean the Other Person Heard It

I described transitioning your thinking as the hard work of Echo Selling because over time, most sellers train themselves to think like salespeople. We must train ourselves to think differently before we can "train" others to echo our words.

Training, to be clear, is practicing. We get really good at whatever we practice. Most salespeople get really good at listening to themselves and other salespeople. Ironically, salespeople don't get as much practice listening to customers, even though they talk to them all the time. Why? Because the truth is most sellers spend far more time each day talking rather than listening.

The way sellers describe their conversation with their customer, especially during pipeline review meetings, lets me know which party the seller was listening to — themselves or the customer.

The stories that sellers tell during pipeline review meetings demonstrates the seller's listening skills. Only the sellers with great listening skills hear the six stories that cover the most common sales meeting "plot lines." If every seller had better listening skills, they could give better, shorter answers in pipeline review meetings. And those meetings would be much shorter AND more productive as a result.

Boiling down your summary description of a sale you are working on, particularly the last conversation you had with the customer, takes practice. You need to practice not getting distracted by what you were trying to tell the customer so you can correctly tune into what really happened.

> **The Takeaway: Sellers need to listen better in order to properly describe their sale during pipeline review meetings. Telling others what you tried to say to the customer is not the same thing as describing how the customer reacted to your words. To get people to echo you, be more aware of their reaction than to your own words.**

The "Usual Suspects": Six Sales Plot Lines That Describe Most Sales Meetings

Over my career I have had the chance to review the sales pipeline of nearly 50,000 salespeople. As a result, I have heard many, many, many sales stories. Well, actually, I've heard all six:

1. The buyer is interested but the timing is wrong.
2. The buyer is interested but they are not the final decision maker. That person can't be reached. Their company has delegated the "shopping" to this buyer.
3. The buyer wants to loop-in their team before they make a decision.
4. The buyer wants to buy, but they need to share costs with another department or two.
5. They would buy now — if it were in the budget.
6. They asked me to send them a proposal.

I wish sellers would describe their opportunities this way: "I just had a meeting. It was #3. I'm going to meet the team next Wednesday."

Instead, their answers devolve into long stories, like " … this one's different. I met the customer, who I *think* is the right person … anyway, they told me they were the right person. So, I told them about our features, then I told them about the benefits, then I told them how other, similar companies already buy from us." You know what I think about while I am listening? So many wasted sales opportunities! All because the salesperson thought what they said was more important than how the customer reacted.

In this story, the salesperson's words are a distraction. At best, what we learn from listening to these stories is how the customer answered the seller's questions.

By reverse engineering the answers, we uncover what the salesperson asked. For example, if the customer said, "we are using your competition, but we hate them!" most salespeople will report the story as "the customer is ready to switch suppliers." I listen to that and come to a very different conclusion. The seller must have asked: "are you happy with the company you are currently using?" The buyer apparently likes the incumbent vendor enough to pay them. Given that reality, what was the point of asking that question? From a game-theory point of view, what did the seller think was a possible answer? Did the salesperson actually think that the customer would say "Every month when we pay their invoice, I pray another salesperson will sell us a much more lovable solution? That is why I was so eager to meet you today!"

The customer's answer should have been "the reason we are currently using the other company is … " That story would have been in response to a better question: "Why are you using the company you are using?" The reason that question is better is it gives the customer an opportunity to explain their current thinking.

> *The Takeaway: Echo Selling relies on creating messaging that dovetails with the customer's way of thinking. Learn what the customer is thinking.*

What Does the Customer Actually Hear?

When we talk to customers during sales meetings, it's tempting to think that the customer is listening to everything they hear, processing everything and remembering the highlights. Why should we expect that when in general, people barely communicate? Most people have an attention span that looks like a sine curve:

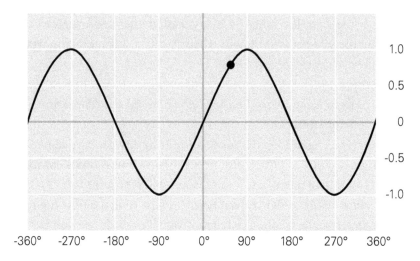

Every time the customer is distracted by something they see or by something else they're thinking about, you can assume their attention span is at the bottom of the curve. Our body language as well as something happening behind us (like something flying past the window) are classic reasons that customers — and salespeople — get distracted. When the customer is at the bottom of their attention curve, they will likely stay there unless and until the salesperson says something relevant — for instance, how their service might help the customer. For this reason, it's more helpful to think of this curve and to keep in mind that gaining and maintaining someone's attention is a constant uphill battle, and not a one-and-done. This will keep you focused on not losing them just as you get to the point you want them to echo.

And, when considering your word choice, remember that we will lose the customer again if they hear a word they don't understand (and don't want to admit to the seller they don't know — after all, no one wants to look foolish). Make sure they understand everything you say.

Think about translating your message. In the same way you would work extra hard to communicate if the other person spoke a different language, consider that even people who speak the same language can easily misunderstand. We need to translate our message to customers who may "speak our language" and "know the business" but still are not on the same page we are on. Always remember:

- The customer knows more than we do
- The customer knows less than we do
- The customer knows less than they think they do

> **The Takeaway: You can lose the customer if you are speaking "over their head," "under their head" or differently than what's in their head. To get on and stay on the same page as the customer, you need to level-set to determine which page they are on relative to the page you are on.**

Your customer is likely echoing someone right now

We need to recognize in the customer's words when they are echoing someone else. To do that, we need to reconsider the conversation we have at the early stage of a sale. Don't try to figure out how you can make the customer think about buying. Instead, figure out what they think about. How do they think about their challenges? How do they view their choice of solutions? What do they do? What do they believe about solutions to their challenges? Their answers are revealed through their stories explaining what they do (if we ask them the right questions). Listen closely when they describe their recent history of solving similar problems and why they do it that way. Clarify what they tell you so you can learn if they are echoing someone else. Go beyond getting answers to questions; get them to reveal where they get their ideas. Learn where they learned the words, phrases, examples and stats that are part of their answers to your questions. Learn who influenced their thinking and why they are echoing their words. Where do they get the information they trust? Who has their ear? Whose opinion do they care about? Unless we understand which messages this person will echo, we'll never get them to echo us.

> **The Takeaway: Don't try to influence the customer's thinking before you learn the customer's current thinking. Listen for what they say so you can learn who gave them their best ideas.**

Echo Selling builds Brand Ambassadors

We are not trying to use echo selling to magically brainwash people. We are not trying to convince anyone of anything. We are not trying to convert everyone into opportunities in your CRM (Salesforce.com for many sellers).

We *are* trying to convert people (customers and their circle of influencers) into brand ambassadors. To get there, we need to communicate in the same way they currently communicate with each other. We need to focus on the impact of our words. When the right words are delivered in the right context, it produces the right imagery in people's heads. When that happens, the customer and their circle of influencers think it was their idea. Brand ambassadors embrace imagery, not words. Branding is when we get customers to see an image and imagine themselves in that image. Brand ambassadors invite others into that image.

> **The Takeaway: Sellers convince by teaching others how the salesperson thinks about solving problems. Brand Ambassadors convey an image that is inviting to others.**

Stop Swimming in Circles

I call it *swimming in circles* when you start every year with the goal of finally have a breakout sales year and end up making about the same number of sales every year.

That circle is the inevitable result of following the same daily patterns, especially the pattern of using the same word choices during common sales situations. There should be no surprise that your end-of-year results are the same when, throughout each year, we follow last year's pattern for how we greet prospects, answer their questions and suggest next steps.

Each day that we repeat those patterns, our comfort level with those patterns increases. To change those patterns, we first need to teach ourselves how to overcome the psychological pain of changing to new patterns. Any change comes with a risk. At worst, risk introduces stress, at best, discomfort. Meanwhile comfort zones exert a gravitational force which pull us back every time we even consider moving away. As a sales trainer, I have learned you can't under-estimate the power of *not changing*.

The first step in changing patterns is changing the questions we ask ourselves, especially this one: "hmm, if I were the customer, what would I like to hear from the salesperson?" The limitation of that question is that it allows salespeople to make any word choice decision they can think of. In the end, the salesperson justifies everything they do, say and write with that excuse.

But when we think *digitally*, we engage customers with messages which are relevant, meaning what a customer is tuning into at any given moment. In the same way that banner ads are relevant and interesting when you are shopping for a service but background noise when you are not, echo sellers engage by keeping their conversation relevant.

Echo sellers ask themselves better questions, like: "What is the customer listening for? Which words will resonate? After I talk to the customer, what will they tell their circle?"

What is relevant to one customer is not always relevant to all. Most sellers guess customers are always thinking about saving money. Digitally thinking echo sellers know that relevance is always changing and adjust their conversations accordingly. As a result, they change their questions, answers, next steps and end-of-year results.

The Takeaway: You can either change the pattern of conversations with customers or expect the same results year over year. To change that pattern, which gets cemented in place over time, change the questions you ask yourself about what the customer is thinking.

The key to making progress: Be honest about your starting point

How would you describe your current "sales conversation preparation" pattern?

Most salespeople are weak at properly preparing *because* they are so practiced in the art of making things up as they get to them. All of that practice has made us feel very confident and comfortable with improvising, but unable to change what we do or the results we get. Why? Because, after you believe you are good at doing anything in a certain way, all other ways feel less comfortable. Most people compound this problem by deciding that discomfort is a sign that they are doing something wrong. That is why we say "this doesn't feel right" just before we stop doing something new and revert back to our old way, which only reinforces our feeling that our original way was right in the first place.

"It doesn't feel right" really means that we have established, unconsciously, our personal set of rules, such as: *always begin prospecting with an email introduction,* or *always begin each meeting by asking "why did you agree to meeting me today?"* or *always conclude the first meeting by promising to send a proposal.*

To learn a new skill, the seller must re-examine their own rules with an open mind. To optimize results of sales conversations, we will need to be more purposeful and less "automatic" in our actions, questions and responses.

Personally, my most important rule is: *always re-audition all sales rules every year.* Which rules are you following? Which were true last year and are still true? How can we all adapt our rules for a changing marketplace with changing technology and expanding communication channels and evolving customer preferences? Which rules will we need to change to avoid swimming in circles?

> *The Takeaway: To change annual results, we need to change our daily patterns, especially our pattern of words choices we make in familiar sales situations. To change "habitual" word choices, we need to recognize and change the underlying rules we created for ourselves and are unconsciously following.*

Break the Gravitational Forces of Resisting Change by Playing to Your Strength

I believe, deep down we would all prefer to avoid any discomfort. When we view certain work-related tasks as uncomfortable, we often work hard to avoid them. But, if we are forced to do those activities a lot, eventually they enter our comfort zone. We now know that our comfort zone is really based on our own set of rules for what feels right. When our rules prevent us from even trying something, like the newest sales-productivity app, we come up with a million reasons why we never even tried it. But, once we learn how to do it well, we view it as playing to our strength. Playing against your strength is hard. Playing to your strength is easy, which is why I describe it as *Lazy* in my book Leverage your Laziness. I don't mean lazy in a judgmental way, but rather as a measure of effort. The "lazy plan" is also the "safest plan" because it involves you doing what you already do well, rather than relying on the things you currently do poorly.

Consider: There are two paths to every goal. One would require you do many things, some of which you are not currently good at or comfortable doing. The other strategy, which would uniquely suit your strengths, would be filled with activities you like doing, are good at and come naturally to you. Which path is more likely going to lead you to success? Your path to success may not be a straight line or the right one for anyone else. But, it's a plan that only requires one thing of you: to do your best at doing the things you like doing, are good at and come naturally to you.

Echo Selling is a great example of Leveraging your Laziness, which is what digital thinkers think of as efficiency, also known as the path of least resistance.

Assume you have to leverage the customer's natural laziness when it comes to making it easy for them to echo. When considering your "meeting talk" and email and document writing, keep asking: *how can I make it easier for the customer to tell (sell) all of their influencers?*

> **The Takeaway: You need to leverage your own laziness when you attempt to change yourself. You need to leverage your customer's natural 'laziness' by making Echo Selling easier for them.**

Deconstructing The Magic of Echo Selling

Salespeople have many more first conversations than closes. For that reason, the first conversation in a sale, by virtue of all that practice, is the hardest part to change. But, only by changing our first conversations can we achieve the magic of Echo Selling.

What is magic? A simple answer is unexplained process. When we don't understand the process, it looks like magic to us. When we watch a magic trick, we are fooled into thinking the magic happened after the trick began. In reality, the magic started *before* the trick began. For example, a person thinks the card trick begins after they selected a "random" card from the face-down cards offered. But in reality, the magician began the trick before they revealed the deck of cards they would be using. Let's apply that to the magic of Echo Selling.

Think of closing the sale as a magic trick. That trick didn't just begin after the seller finished Qualifying, Gaining Information, Presenting and Negotiating. The closing "trick" began unseen by the customer, during the preparation phase before the first meeting.

There are four things you need to know about preparing for sales meetings, five if you count the fact that most salespeople hate to practice sales conversations. I'll summarize each here and we'll analyze them individually over the next few chapters:

1. You need to separate out the word choice from the delivery; that is, first come up with what you want to say. Then, in a separate part of the practice, you need to prepare to say those words. (For this reason, we've broken the preparation process into three parts — structure, word choice selection and performance tips).

2. Practicing the art of saying what you want to say is a skill that we often skip because we think we are already good at *the talking part* of sales. (we'll explore the psychological "optical illusions" which skew our perception about what really works and what doesn't in the upcoming chapter, Rehearsing Real Conversations).

3. To learn something new we need to first overcome or offset the momentum created by the things we practice the most. For most salespeople, the thing we practice the most is selling without practice. Training isn't what happens in a twice-a-year workshop; it's what you practice each day. (We explore this concept in the next chapter called Convince Yourself That Preparation Is Better Than Winging It.)

4. It is uncomfortable when we change the way we do things that we do all the time. Therefore, to change anything in life in general and sales in particular, we need to change the way we feel about being uncomfortable. (We'll explore the three kinds of discomfort we need to confront and overcome in the chapter called: How Swimming the English Channel Made Me A Better Salesperson).

> ***The Takeaway: We can't properly Echo Sell until we properly practice and prepare. To do that, we need to learn (or re-learn) how to practice and prepare.***

Convince Yourself That Preparation Is Better Than Winging It.

The biggest mistake I see salespeople make is under-preparing for things they plan on improvising. We fool ourselves into believing *winging it* will work, even though logic says otherwise.

We are all prone to getting fooled by an "optical illusion" that psychologists call availability heuristics. A heuristic is the technical term for a "gut feeling." We are fooled by our own gut feeling that something is true if we can easily remember it happening (when we reach into our memory, it's easily available). So, if I can easily remember one instance when I was brave, I believe I am brave. If I easily remember one time I was clumsy in front of a crowd of others, I believe I am clumsy. Even though people say it often rains in Seattle, I've been there six times and it never rained when I was there. So, I guess it doesn't rain there a lot, right?

Of course, looking up the data would solve the question "scientif-ically." But, we all tend to first use our gut feeling, because it is easier. Even if we look it up, we tend to be fooled by *confirmation bias*, which is the preference to only believe and see the things we already believe to be true.

When it comes to analyzing what works, we could use our gut feeling (psychologists call this form of decision-making System 1) or we could analyze data (System 2). Humans have evolved to gravitate toward System 1 whenever possible. During our caveman days, that saved us from being eaten by larger animals *(what's that noise behind that big rock? Safer to flee than to delay while analyzing all of the data!)* And since salespeople tend to be terrible at record keeping, we've evolved to be better at following our gut than analyzing our data, when trying to determine what works best.

Assume the customer will use their System 1 thinking when making their first impression of us; meanwhile, many salespeople use System 1 thinking to decide on the spot what to say to them. Make sure you are properly prepared for a great first meeting by using System 2 thinking during your meeting preparation.

> *The Takeaway: Salespeople tend to be overly influ-enced by famous exceptions. We remember the one time some sales "trick" worked. We forget the 1,000 times it didn't work. This is a huge problem for sales-people because we are always trying to answer the*

question "does it work when I do this?" As a result, people who improv their way through sales conversations will remember the one time they were great under pressure more easily than they will recall the many times preparation would have helped.

Customers are people, too

Psychology misleads the customer, too.

The expression "don't judge a book by its cover" is great advice but few people are following it. Famously, publishing companies spend more money on the cover than the rest of the book because the cover is the way most people can (and will) judge a book.

Is that fair? Is that right? Of course not! But, that doesn't stop customers and others from being fooled by the Halo Effect. That's when we ascribe to strangers the same range of qualities we associate with people we know who share one similarity. For example, if a stranger has a voice that is similar to our funny friend, we think the stranger will be funny. If the boss once had a great employee who was very tall, they may think a tall applicant would also make a great employee. This can lead to both positive and negative results — for example, when a person meets a someone who reminds them of someone they don't like.

Salespeople need to think about this when they meet new customers. Sometimes the customer thinks the new salesperson reminds them of another salespeople who annoyed them or was otherwise unhelpful, based on one similar attribute — like a "salesy" elevator pitch. In that case, that salesperson must work twice as hard to get the customer to like them. Why work so hard? Because people buy with their emotions; they will more likely buy from a salesperson they like.

Who is your customer comparing you to when they are developing their first impression about you? Assume your customer uses their availability heuristic gut feeling to unscientifically (and unfairly) jump to a conclusion.

This is why I always ask my new customers about their experience with previous sales trainers.

I recommend that Account Managers learn the customer's feelings about the service teams from the other services they buy from. Aim to be your customer's favorite AM. Try to find a comfortable way of asking: *Please tell me what you liked most about the best ones so I can emulate that behavior* (or words to that effect). I tell my customers *I want to be the one they compare all other salespeople to* (of course I say that with a half-smile, hoping they associate a sense of humor with people they like being with).

Salespeople need to act in a certain way based on the customer's feelings about other salespeople in their lives. To simplify this concept, think about the last salesperson the customer dealt with.

From a game-theory point of view, which is to consider all possibilities when deciding what to do next, you have to make one of two assumptions:

- The previous salesperson was annoying, and the customer will *confuse* me for that person unless I actively and deliberately act completely differently. In that case, it would give me a strategic advantage to thoroughly prepare for every meeting.

- The previous salesperson was great at reassuring customers with caring and insightful questions and perfect answers. In that case, it obligates me to perfect my sales conversation through careful preparation, so the customer thinks as highly of me as they think of the other salesperson ... who they find so easy to remember whenever they think of examples of great salespeople they have met in their lives.

The Takeaway: Preparation gives you a strategic advantage not only for the obvious, logical reasons but for the not-so-obvious psychological reason of human nature.

Learning To Remove the Need For An Excuse

I've heard the word "excuse" defined as a well-planned lie. If you convince yourself before a meeting that there are multiple reasons why the sale won't close (i.e., *the competition has lower prices*), then two things will happen: you won't properly prepare ("excuse") and you'll blame something other than yourself when the sale indeed does *not* close ("lie").

I have had two experiences in my life that caused me to think of excuses as a safety net. Both made me wonder: what if I live my life without the safety net of excuses? I would approach the goal of being successful differently than most people, who believe that positive thinking is all that is needed. The most successful people get there by focusing on preventing failure.

Let me show you how my experiences as both an improvisational actor, and an open water swimmer facing life-threatening events, have taught me how to properly train for sales meetings.

> **The Takeaway: If you are open to learning, you will find lots of things that have nothing to do with sales but will teach you how to be a better salesperson.**

Improvisation Takes Practice

I was a member of the First Amendment, a top NYC improv group, in my younger days. Robin Williams performed with us when he was in town. Writers from Saturday Night Live came to our performances. We once did a private show for Barbara Streisand.

I thought the audition to get into the group would be a mere formality. I already knew how to do improv, having previously performed with another group. But the NYC group only accepted me if I first joined their workshop to study the art of professional improv for a year. *What? But, I already know how to do improv!* (By the way, notice how similar this reaction is to the one most sellers give when told they need to attend sales training).

During that year, I learned the meaning of professional improv. It's not only that the actors get paid; it means the paying customers expect each show to be funny. It's relatively easy to be funny some or even most of the time, especially when working with a talented group of people. But, to be funny every single show, you had to prevent any bit from being *not funny*.

There's a concept in the world of improv known as "Yes! And..." This is the rule of agreeing with the other person so you can create a scene together by building on each other's contributions. But it is more like three-dimensional chess when you reverse-engineer scenes to see what you need to *avoid* doing.

For example, a common first reaction to the audience's suggestion is to launch into a "teaching scene." That is, take a suggestion such as *fishing* and begin by saying "*ok, little brother, let me teach you how to catch a shark.*" While that is easy to fall into, teaching scenes invariably lead to not-funny scenes. I spent a year learning what to do and what to avoid doing in order to consistently achieve funny results. We performed in front of a paying audience on the weekends but rehearsed at least five nights every week in advance. While each show was indeed improvised, the process we followed made us fool-proof. No matter how different each night's audience was, no matter how bizarre any suggestion was, we knew what to do — and what to avoid doing — in order to give every member of the audience their money's worth every performance.

Selling is like improv, except that our customers pay us only after they are happy with our performance. Given that, what is your approach to practice? Are you spending five times more time in practice versus your performance time? Or are you using improv without first considering how to reverse engineer failed sales conversations?

> *The Takeaway: Statistically, even the best salespeople mostly don't succeed. Even if you close 1 in 3 sales, which would be amazingly good, you still don't win 2 out of 3 times. And, in today's world, it's harder than ever to get even one meeting. Given that, we can't let anything slip through our fingers without first doing everything possible to make sure it goes well. This especially applies to introductory sales conversations with each new contact.*

How Swimming the English Channel Made Me A Better Salesperson

I swam competitively from 6th grade through college. Then, several years ago, after a long layoff, I agreed to join some friends in an open water swimming relay around the island of Manhattan. The thrill of completing that race led our team captain to suggest: "Next year, the English Channel!"

More people have gotten to the top of Mount Everest than have successfully swum the Channel.

When I was competing in college, I thought of workouts as something your coach made you do. But when I was preparing for the English Channel, I was trying not to die. If my competitors beat me in the pool, I always had a ready excuse: *what can you do? Maybe they were faster than me?* But in the English Channel it didn't matter what excuse I could come up with. Unless I was ready, I would die, which was something I learned from reading the medical release form they make you sign before they allow you to swim.

With that as a starting point, I began to think of the things that could go wrong, namely cold water, rough water and jellyfish.

I could imagine the cold water alone would make me want to give up, especially because the water in the English Channel is 50-55° Fahrenheit. And, it's against their rules to swim with a wet suit. All you get to wear is a short speedo swimsuit, goggles and one bathing cap. They actually check to make sure you don't have two.

The rough water is due to the fact that you have to swim East for more than 20 miles against a fast current which alternates between going North and South. The only way to make forward progress is to do a giant S shape. The current is especially fast the final mile going into France and it is the main reason that five out of six solo swimmers don't make it.

But of all the potential excuses, my biggest personal challenge was dealing with a fear of jellyfish. Jellyfish, and other marine life, freak me out. And if I encountered a school of them in my path, I would have to swim through them.

I trained by envisioning the worst-case scenario over and over again.

Since I was worried about becoming exhausted, I'd swim long two-part workouts to improve my endurance. The first part was designed to exhaust me. Then, I'd sprint as fast as I could as long as could after I was already tired.

I spent hours swimming into rough water until I could figure out how to do it. The team swam for four hours in jellyfish infested waters the week prior to the English Channel swim until we had a million stings, but knew we would survive them. By creating workouts that replicated and exaggerated the worst-case scenarios I could imagine encountering, I was able to swim even though I was fearful.

After a year and a half of training, I still wasn't able to *not* be afraid, but I was not going to be stopped by any of the harsh conditions. I knew the other relay team members trained with that mindset, too. We made it in 14 hours and 28 minutes!

The lesson I learned: practice isn't "check the box." Practice only helps if you put yourself into the worst-case scenario. When applied to sales, normal practice includes looking over your presentation. English Channel-style practice assumes that the other person will be either uninterested or will have a lot of objections. They will surprise you by telling you they only have five minutes. Your presentation technology won't work and you will have to present without it. The harder you make the role play, the less likely you will fail in real life.

> *The Takeaway: Success doesn't result from merely thinking positive thoughts. It comes by eliminating failure. Success in sales isn't about what you know. It's about what you do. Successful salespeople do the things everyone else just talks about, but are unwilling to do ... like really scripting, then personalizing and practicing their elevator pitch in rough water, with their teammates watching.*

Successful Echo Selling is the by-product of word choice preparation that follows digital thinking.

Echo sellers are driven to make the most of each sales interaction. Echo sellers develop the ability to diagnose sales conversations — their own and others they observe — for its potential to create the right impression and provide the right words to echo. They learn to identify weak parts in their own communication. They strengthen them with the right preparation, which we will describe in Part 3 — Word Choice and Performance Tips.

> *The Takeaway: Successful Echo Selling is only possible with the right thinking and preparation.*

Selling your Brand

Consider how much branding advertising influences you in a supermarket, a car dealer, a liquor store and everywhere else you shop. You will go to several stores — or websites - to find exactly what you want — even though you may not be able to articulate why that brand has such power over you.

Echo selling advertises your brand. This eventually leads to sales because it changes the way the customer *thinks and feels* about your brand. But it only works if you communicate the right message in the right way at the right time.

We'll breakdown the keys to Echo Selling messaging into what you say and how you say it (aka, word choice and performance tips) in Part 3. We'll tackle message timing, which we call Echo Selling campaign execution, in Part 4.

> *The Takeaway: To successfully echo sell, you need to change the way customers think and feel about your brand. To do that, you need to say the right thing in the right way at the right time on the right platform.*

Echo Selling Word Choice and Performance Tips

Prepare to be Relevant by Developing Answers to the Five Most Essential Customer Questions

Customers, including salespeople when they are buying, aren't really hearing everything the salesperson says. Why? Because customers are listening for the salesperson's answer to these five questions:

1. What do you sell which is relevant to helping me (the customer)?
2. What makes your (the salesperson's) offer different from others who claim to do similar things?
3. What is the advantage of working with you / your company?
4. What makes your offer worth the investment (ROI+)?
5. Why do you think you and your company are right for us?

The message that we want others to echo is the answers to these five seemingly easy-to-answer questions.

> *The Takeaway: The customer already has five essential questions in their head. They won't move to the next step of recommending us to others until they are reassured by our answers. The job of the Echo Salesperson is to help them remember our answers so they can repeat them to themselves and their circle of influencers.*

The Questions Behind the Questions Your Customer Really Wants You To Answer

To simplify the process of developing the right messaging, I've broken down the five most essential questions to reveal what the customer really wants to know ...

Prepare to answer this customer question	Unasked Questions: What the customer really wants to know
What do you sell which is relevant to helping me?	a. *Convince me that you/your company is credible.* b. *Then explain the problem we have that your solution addresses better than our current method.* c. *If I have to explain your offering to a co-worker, what can I tell them about you that makes me look good for talking to you about potential solutions?*
What makes your offer different from others who claim to do similar things?	a. *How are your differences a better fit for me?* b. *If I have to talk to a co-worker about changing vendors, which of your differences can I share that makes me look smart for finding you?*
What is the advantage of working with you / your company?	a. *Why would a customer, like me, work with you?* b. *When I tell a co-worker why I am interested in learning more about you, I need a story I can share that will inspire them too.*
What makes your offer worth the investment (ROI+)?	a. *How do I make more money/reduce my costs more if I buy from you?* b. *If I have to defend the budget to someone else, what can I tell them?*
Why do you think you and your company are right for us?	a. *You (the salesperson) know your own company and presumably know us. Given all of that insight, what is the logic behind your thinking that we should work together?* b. *Can you give me a compelling reason that I can share with my circle (boss, team, peers) why they should think about buying from you?*

> *The Takeaway: your answers need to address the customer's unasked questions, too.*

Selecting the right words when there is so much to communicate

Seemingly easy to answer questions can take smart people all day to answer. To make Echo-able, separate out what you want to say from how you say it.

I have worked with thousands of companies to help them develop their answers to these questions. I've watched experienced salespeople - and even experienced sales managers — struggle with this exercise. The problem is we have too much understanding of how our solution fits. We know too much about the customers we want to sell to. There are too many possible ways to describe what we want to say.

And, while delivering answers, the seller needs to consider their own body language, non-verbal communication and current relationship with the customer to properly nuance their answer — at just the right time in a conversation, like a professional pool player putting just the touch on the ball to make an impossible shot look easy.

Remember: People barely communicate. We need to consider what we are saying versus what the other person hears. Expect "uneven listening" caused by wandering attention spans and subliminal distractions of body language and non-verbal communication.

Now you understand why answering these questions are *seemingly* easy. In fact, now that I have listed the challenges, you realize getting someone to echo our thoughts is hard. It's for this reason that I have developed this 3-part approach to preparation:

1. Structure — Putting your words into the right structure makes listening and understanding easier for the customer.
2. Word choice — Selecting the right words helps you "translate" and personalize your message for every customer.
3. Performance tips — People remember how you said something more easily than they remember what you said.

> *The Takeaway: To make it easy for customers to tell their circle about you, think about what they are listening for, what you are going to say and how you are going to say it.*

Answering Question #1 - What do you sell? And how is it relevant to helping a particular customer?

Let's begin developing an answer to this critical question by starting at a very high-level. In this chapter, we'll look at the structure of your answer from 30,000 feet.

This is the first answer you need to develop; it's the bedrock of all Echo-able messages. The answer is your elevator pitch. Well, maybe not your current pitch, but that pitch is the placeholder for this answer. To create the right answer, start by remembering our two "unasked" questions:

a. What is our customer actively listening for?

b. Who will they tell / What will they say to their circle if they found what they are listening for?

(Hint: To answer those questions, you may need to first learn: Where have they been looking so far in their search for a potentially helpful solution? How long they've been looking? What do they need to learn to feel reassured that the salesperson is in fact relevant, unique and worth the investment of their time, attention and money?

Your elevator pitch needs to address these unasked questions:

a. Convince me that you/your company is credible.

b. Then explain the problem we have that your solution addresses better than our current method.

c. If I have to explain your offering to a co-worker, what can I tell them about you that makes me look good for talking to you about potential solutions?

One last thing to remember before you write (or re-write) your elevator pitch. What is the purpose of an elevator pitch? Is it only to answer their questions about us? Actually, our goal is to deliver answers that encourage your customer to answer more of our questions.

When your meetings end with a next step, it's not luck. The customer chose you. They heard from you what they need to tell the next person about you.

> **The Takeaway: The customer is already looking for certain answers and reassurances. Develop your answer from the customer's point of view, not the salesperson's. Make it easy for customers to tell their circle about you.**

The real reason for the elevator pitch

Now let's take a closer look at the structure of an Echo-able Elevator Pitch.

If we do the Elevator Pitch right, we'll make it as easy as possible for the customer to see in us what they are looking for as well as how to answer questions about us that their circle will ask.

The best way to deliver that pitch: Be clear. Reduce the wording. Deliver the information in the order the customer is listening for. Bullet points work best. Consider formatting your answer into three or four sentences but begin the brainstorming by focusing on short phrases and keywords.

Your pitch should sound like you are trying to help the customer, with the fewest number of words, understand what you can do for them. Ideally, you need two versions — the long version (60-90 seconds) that you'll use in sales meetings. And the short version (5-10 seconds) you will use when prospecting and networking.

The best way to reduce the word count is to pump up the imagery with an apt metaphor.

By referring to the metaphor early on in your elevator pitch, you are encouraging the customer to view the remaining parts of your elevator pitch through the right lens.

So, your elevator pitch should be structured like this:

We are... (the description of company's category — what kind of company are you?)

We do... (the services you provide)

*We are like _____(metaphor)

We solve these problems ... (the problems you solve, the resources. products, services and solutions you combine to solve customer problems)

We work with customers like (examples of "relevant" others, organized by company size or another trait)

" ... and, my role and background is ... " (optional final part, if the seller is professionally credible independent of the credibility of their team, such as a 15-year industry veteran, or experience on the customer side).

*When the salesperson says their service is like _____ (name of another famous company, product or solution), you are simultaneously giving them your message in the fewest number of words and providing them with an echo-able message.

Consider if you don't provide a metaphor. The customer may think of their own which may not be as flattering as the one you wish they chose. For example, you may think your service is as hot as a habanero pepper, but without your metaphor guidance the customer may describe your service to others as *plain vanilla*.

> **The Takeaway: Provide your customer with the right metaphor rather than force your customer to remember everything you said – or worse - think of their own metaphor when describing you to their circle of influencers.**

Versions of the elevator pitch

Choosing The Right Words to Translate Your Message

It turns out that you need to translate even when the other person speaks the same language you do, because the customer either knows more than you, less than you or less than they think they know. It's like three different languages.

Each person will engage with - or ignore certain things you say - depending on which language they speak. For example, you can lose a person who knows less than you if you use technical terms. Even before they ask you to explain, they'll tune out.

But, you may appear lacking in credibility if you don't use technical terms when talking to a person who knows more than you.

For this reason, you must level-set first. For example, when I was in the digital marketing business, I asked each prospect about their "CPA metric" which is "digital marketing speak" for the amount of marketing money a company will pay for each sale (conversion). The expression is well known to very hands-on marketing managers and not well understood by anyone else. So, I'd innocently ask about the customer's *CPA metric* at the start of every meeting just to see how they reacted. When they were unfamiliar, I'd simplify my words accordingly.

The more technical your sale, the bigger the gap between what the salesperson means and what the customer hears. To simplify the problem of translating, use Plain Speak, which is the common language all three groups speak.

Don't aim to impress with how smart you are. It won't impress at least two of the three kinds of customers you will meet. Instead, impress "by accident" by finding novel ways to describe complex problems and solutions using familiar, clear, unambiguous words and phrases. For example, consider how "A better mouse trap" is a better way to describe anti-virus software, than using some technical term known only to software engineers if talking to non-engineer business leaders.

Your word choice, and not the overall intent of your message, is what persists in people's memory. Translating the message ensures — or at least encourages the other person to pay attention to you, which is the key to them even hearing your word choice.

> *The Takeaway: Anyone can learn to describe a complex solution using complex language. It says so much more about your confidence and competence when you use Plain Speak when describing complex ideas. By using Plain Speak, the salesperson suggests how much value they will bring by how simply they see complex problems and how plainly they see the needed solution.*

To Perfect the Perfect Answer, *Discover* an Echo-Able Elevator Pitch During Practice

The quest for the perfectly worded elevator pitch is a great example of *perfection being the enemy of good.*

Your goal is to get the same enthusiastic reaction from different people. It's not to use the same elevator pitch with everyone.

You learn through role play with peers how different people may react to your message. Practice changing their reaction by changing what and how you deliver your pitch.

> **The Takeaway: Role play practice is the best way to develop the skill of talking while paying attention to the other person's reaction. Echo Sellers learn to adjust their words to get the desired reaction.**

Finding The Right Words and Sentence Order: The Art and Science of Scripting

To the customer, your elevator pitch is a story about you.

The trick is to get the facts about your company and offering to sound like a great story that keeps the listener engaged. To get there, you need more than simply repeating the same pitch until you can say it in your sleep (in other words, standard sales training). It takes scripting, even though the goal is to sound unscripted.

Keep in mind people's level of attention changes throughout the day and during the course of each meeting. To regain lost attention spans, consider the order you tell your elevator pitch "story."

Scripting will force you to use short sentences. It will encourage *Plain speak* and help you notice and avoid all of the industry jargon and initials you may unconsciously add.

My advice: Don't begin with features or benefits. Start with "people proof," which is how your benefits have helped similar customers. In coming up with your script, consider what problems you helped your customers solve. If you have been with your company a long time, make sure to work yourself into that script. How many companies have you helped?

I find that writing and re-writing my elevator pitch allows me to discover the many choices I hadn't really thought about. For example: how few words I really need. How much I could leave out. The parts I should emphasize. The many ways I could make it better. Apart from word-choice, play with the order of names, facts and figures. Find the most easily remembered order which usually is small to large (for example "we have partnered with 50 clients to execute 1,000 campaigns annually, reaching 1,000,000 targeted leads every week.)

Keep in mind the answer the customer or prospect is listening for: they want reassurance that you are potentially worth their time. And, if they like what they hear, we have to make it easy for them to tell others.

> **The Takeaway: When you script what you want to say, you let yourself view the words in a format perfect for identifying the many things you could change to improve. Two benefits of re-writing the script is that it helps you develop it into the way you talk rather than the way you write ... and all of that repetition will help you memorize it.**

Customer-forward writing style

Always remember people's constantly wandering attention span. The only way not to lose people is to keep your elevator pitch interesting, by making it relevant to them.

> **The Takeaway: Your elevator pitch works best and is most easily repeated when the listener hears something that sounds to them like: You sell a solution that fits the customer's needs like a "key-in-a-lock"/ "hand-in-a-glove" / "Use-case story in a nutshell."**

The Only Safe Assumption in Sales: Assume You Will Need Another Way to Word Something

I worried just now that I lost you when I recommended you script your elevator pitch. I know what you are thinking ... *scripting is bad.*

I don't want my elevator pitch to sound scripted. Don't worry, it won't. In the same way that actors begin with scripts but make their words sound conversational with a lot of practice (rehearsal), your elevator pitch will sound unrehearsed and make a bigger impact as a result of all of that practice.

If possible, script it with team members or trusted friends. Start with a brain dump before trying to polish each sentence. Capture the complete list of everything you do to help every kind of customer you service. Don't worry about redundancies.

Here's a case where you have to stop thinking like an insecure salesperson and leverage your laziness by thinking like a confident improvisation actor who is trained to say "yes, and … ."

Brainstorm the complete list of your features and benefits plus your mission and your promise to the marketplace. How do you know when you have enough stuff? You need enough to answer *What do you sell?* in a series of role plays where the answer is delivered to every kind of lead (character) you expect to talk to. Do you have enough things to say and enough ways to say it to "conversationally" answer this question translated to every kind of customer?

The only way to know is do lots of role play practice. Role plays, especially when done in front of peers, develops the most important skill: The ability to deliver under pressure. This means being purposeful even when you are stressed. In real life, you need to get the words out of your mouth while facing the customer (or your webcam). There's more pressure doing that than reading your answers from a script by yourself with nobody watching.

> **The Takeaway: You prepare to be your best when you practice dealing with the worst things that can happen. By allowing your role plays to flex your "translation" and "plain speaking" muscles, especially in front of a tough audience, you will be ready to be purposeful in every real conversation.**

Rehearse Fitting Your Answer To *'What Do You Sell?'* Into Real Conversations

If you deliver a great elevator pitch before you ask the customer about their needs you'll get better information from them.

But they won't hear your answer unless you first get their attention. And you'll get less information if you deliver your elevator pitch too late into the conversation.

To get this right:

- Start the meeting by exchanging pleasantries

- Ask something about the customer, where you could potentially find something in common (nothing greases the wheels of a conversation better than building on a commonality — especially when the thing in common is that you both know the same person, both used to work for the same company or industry, both are active in the same activity. *A caution here: when the buyer is 30 years older than the seller, it doesn't help to point out you both went to the same high school or college or that your parents bought a home in the same town the buyer now lives in. Instead, find something you currently share in common*).

- And then ask something like "how about if I tell you a little bit about me, you tell me a little bit about you and let's see if we are a good fit for each other." Pause until they agree.

Now they are ready to hear you. And, when you go first, you will make it easier for them to give you the information you want.

> ### The Takeaway: Echo selling requires we have their attention before giving them a potentially echo-able message they will find relevant.

The Psychology of Echo Selling Follows Ingrained "Social Rules" For First Conversations

Salespeople are often taught to hold off on their elevator pitch until the customer explains what they are looking for. But social rules, which are hard-wired communication principles we all tend to follow, requires that the salesperson introduces themselves first — but only after you have their attention.

Let me illustrate this to you by asking you to consider a common social situation where you meet a stranger. Picture you are walking alone in a park and decide to sit down on a park bench to observe the beauty around you. Soon, another person sits down on a nearby bench. Nothing in their demeanor or body language suggests they prefer to be left alone. If your goal is to strike up a conversation, you can easily begin by observing "beautiful day for a walk in the park." Not only is that an innocent meeting & greeting comment, it also serves as a point of commonality, the necessary first step for the social dance of beginning a conversation. The other person picks up on that thread with a rejoinder "I especially love walking in this park this time of year when the leaves are turning."

If I blurt out the question "hey, where were you born?" too early in that conversation, it might turn off the other person who may be wondering why I want to know. They may be thinking "who's asking? Why do you need to know?" Socially, it's easier for the other person to answer if I reveal the same thing about myself first, as in: "most of the people I meet here are from somewhere else. I was born in Brooklyn. Where were you born?"

Let's apply this to a sales conversation. There are two problems with insisting the customer goes first. The first is that it is often given by trainers who memorized a training program but who don't actually sell (I do!). The second is that it fails to consider the psychology of the moment. The customer knows that talking can cost them money in terms of their revealing too great a need or too urgent a timetable or too big a budget. Customers are there to hear the seller talk. Plus, when we go first, we model for the buyer how to summarize a company and a person into a 60-second description.

And when our elevator pitch leaves the customer thinking "wow, this person sounds exactly right for us!" then the customer is more inclined to share helpful information when it's their turn and will give better answers to the salesperson's questions. So, delivering a better elevator pitch early on in the meeting leads to better qualifying.

> *The Takeaway: The often-minimized elevator pitch can help us qualify better if we position it right.*

Before we begin: Set-up your elevator pitch for success

I often begin meetings with the words "before we begin" which suggests that there will be an official beginning, but we are not there yet. Until then, we are relaxed and "off the record." During that "unofficial" moment, I usually ask the customer how long they've been at their company, what were they doing before and how did they get from there to here. Getting the customer to talk is the point of sales conversations. Their answers help me think of *commonalities*. Those are the things we both know, activities we both enjoy and people we know in common. That helps me understand them even before the meeting begins.

People react in kind. If you show an interest in really listening to them, they will listen better to you. I mention this because the promise of Echo Selling, which is to get inbound leads from people who heard about you indirectly through a circle of influencers, can work like a magic trick. But the trick only works at 50% strength when you don't execute the steps correctly. Well before you can get someone to echo your elevator pitch, you need to get their attention. To do that, give them yours.

> *The Takeaway: Get customers to talk before you try to teach them about you and your products and services. Listening to them first makes it easier for them to pay attention and echo your sales pitch.*

Question #2: Now the Fun Begins

In thinking about the questions in every customer's head, so far we've only answered the first one: what do you sell? It turns out that was the easiest question to answer. We analyzed what it takes to prepare and deliver a great elevator pitch. Now, let's analyze the other four questions beginning with: What makes you different?

> *The Takeaway: Let's apply that same analysis (psychology behind the question, the structure of the answer, the word choice selection and performance tips) to the "differences" question.*

They Say That Every Snowflake Is Unique, But They Look the Same to Me: X ≠ Y

Experienced customers eventually conclude that companies in the same business all sound the same.

Why? As humans, we are hard-wired to understand each new thing by first comparing it to something we already know, like algebra. We see X and say this X is like another X we once saw. Then, as we gain more information, we change the formula in our head to: this X looks like old X plus A. Eventually we realize that X+A can't be the same as X, it must be Y; Y and X are different. But the initial feeling that they are the same persists until we are sold on how different they really are.

> *The Takeaway: Humans are programmed to mentally put like things together. Salespeople need to remind themselves of this tendency when they attempt to parse their company from similar competitors in their customer's head.*

Separating Your Company From Your Competitors To Answer The Unasked Question Behind: 'What Makes Us Different?'

Let's remind ourselves of the unasked questions behind the big question:

- *How are your differences a better fit for me?*
- *If I have to talk to a co-worker about changing vendors, which of your differences can I share that makes me look smart for finding you?*

Your answer needs to satisfy the question and unasked questions to be easily echoed.

Implicit in the Big Question (what makes you different) is the understanding that customers expect others (their circle) to also need help seeing the differences. To be satisfied with your answer, they have to be satisfied that their circle will accept your answer, too.

Now that we understand why the customer needs so much help untangling us from our competition, we understand the resistance to seeing — and accepting - our differences. It will take work, in the form of careful preparation, to overcome that mental resistance.

> ***The Takeaway: Salespeople never confuse their own company with the competition, but the customer often does. Remember that completely different mindset when preparing your list of differences.***

The Psychology - And Importance - Behind the Question: What Makes Your Offer Different From Others Who Claim To Do Similar Things?

Before we zero in on the specific word choice needed to make your answer echo-able, let's consider the question from the buyer's point of view.

The most important and common thing to remember about customers: Analysis Paralysis. When customers have too many choices they decide not to decide.

This may explain why some customers seem to be stuck even though the seller delivered a proposal with compelling benefits. Today's customers are buried in similar sounding sales messages from salespeople all over the world who all seem to be saying: *Buy from us because our proven approach is better for you, cost-effective and worth the investment.*

The Halo Effect makes some customers unable to tell the difference between you and your competitors (that is, your book and all the others with similar covers). Customers are thinking "I can't see any differences! I assume there are none — except maybe the price."

Let's also consider the completely different risk levels for customers and salespeople. Sellers are naturally risk tolerant. Customers are risk averse. They are currently buying some services, using internal resources for others and not investing in other things. The buyer is thinking change presents the risk of something going wrong. The seller is saying: change is a safe bet; the benefits will prove worth it.

For this reason, it favors sellers if the market conditions change in a way that force risk-averse customers to bite their lip, hold their nose, take a chance and buy something. For example, new regulations can make companies that would otherwise not invest in anything suddenly rethink their investment strategy. But absent those changing market conditions, the salesperson needs to demonstrate that change is not only potentially beneficial, but actually less risky than not changing.

> *The Takeaway: Learning how you are different in a world where all of the sellers seem to be selling the same solution is the most important part – and the hardest part of the sales process– for salespeople and for customers. Make it easy for the customer who can easily confuse your service for another.*

If You Only Work on One Answer This Year, Make It What Makes You Different?

Of the five questions, this one is possibly the most important one to focus on because both the question and the opportunity to provide the answer come up many times during the sales process.

Putting in the effort to prepare and deliver the best answer will change your sales conversations and your income.

The answer to "what makes you different" can come up early and late in a sale.

Let's start with early in the first meeting of the sale. During that exchange, the customer might mention that they are talking to or already working with the ABC company (competitor of yours). Simply ask:

Seller: Do you know how we are different from ABC?

Customer: No, I thought you were all the same.

Seller: Would it help you if I told you the differences between us and our competitors?

Customer: Sure!

Seller: Well, there are five ways we are different ...

Later on in the sales process your main contact introduces you to a new key stakeholder. Expect the other person to ask: "are you like _____?" by saying something like "well, we are actually different from ___ in five ways … " you'll help them understand who to compare you to — and who you shouldn't be compared with.

The answer comes up again during the negotiation:

Consider the moment the customer looks at your proposal. Their face says "Gee, that's a lot of money."

Then they say: "Gee, the price, the price, the price is a bit, umm, higher than I thought it would be."

Armed with the answer, you can avoid unnecessarily discounting. Instead, steer the conversation in a more helpful direction by asking "What did you think it would be?" Expect the rest of the conversation to go like this:

Customer: About 20% lower.

Seller: Really? Where did you get the number?

Customer: That's what the ABC company is charging.

Seller: Oh … that explains it. Do you know the differences between ABC and us? Would it help you if I told you the five differences?

> *The Takeaway: Having the perfect answer to this question in your back pocket, mentally, during every sales conversation will correctly encourage you to pull it out and use it to best advantage throughout the sales process.*

Everyone Touts Their Differences - Except the Incumbent Vendor

In general, change favors the salesperson. If anything is changing, it might be a time for customers to re-examine all of their vendor relationships. That potentially creates an opportunity for the seller who is trying to break into the customer's short list of vendors. However, if you are the incumbent vendor, a time of change necessitates your developing an entire sales strategy around the question "how are you different?"

If you are the current incumbent vendor, after a while, your being tried-and-true becomes a tired slogan compared to the message of the competing vendor who promises to be the shiny new object, which can be distracting to the most vocal members of the customers circle of influencers.

For both the hunter (seller of the new service) and farmer (incumbent vendor), answering *what are the differences* is not only an opportunity to define the border lines separating you from your competitors. You must also use your answer to address how your differences make you a better choice because you are the safest choice for that customer.

> *The Takeaway: Use your answer to What Makes You Different to paint your offer as the safer bet.*

Explain Why Your Differences Are Important

When your answer is relevant to the customer they may explain why: "It's funny you would mention that. We were just talking about that." But if they don't volunteer that explanation, you need to be prepared to explain why you thought the differences you cited would be relevant.

To be ready for every conversation, always have a reason for mentioning every difference. For example, *"the first difference is our 'punctuality,' which is the newest standard in our industry. Our punctuality rate is the highest because we take advantage of these latest trends ... The reason I thought you would want to know is your counterparts at other companies are telling us that is the biggest issue they face."*

Behind every sound decision is a boatload of psychology which enables buyers to rationalize any decision. Make your list of differences easy for the customer to match up to the trends they are likely hearing about in their internal talk. When there's a match, it's easier for the customer to rationalize defending the decision to care about your solution.

> *The Takeaway: Salespeople need to provide a list of differences that match up with problems, issues and / or challenges those customers are currently discussing with their circle.*

Answer The Question, Literally

Tell, don't sell! Many salespeople I meet conflate *differences* with *advantages*. As a result, they spin their answer to this question (sell). Ironically, your answer is much more persuasive when you actively avoid spinning (tell).

My favorite example of this came from my recent experience in a sporting goods store. I saw two identical looking racquets, one marked $15 and the other $150. I thought it might be an error — maybe they forgot to mark-down one of the racquets? So I asked a salesperson what was the difference between these racquets. His answer was pure spin: "In sports equipment, usually the more expensive something is, the better it is!" Unsatisfied, I asked if there was another salesperson I could speak to. The second salesperson told me the differences in a way that led me to rationalize buying the more expensive racquet. He told me to hold both racquets. "There are ten differences," he said and then pointed out each (the weight, strings, handle, etc.) Each time I asked why that difference was significant, his answer boiled down to: *That difference makes the racquet hit the ball in way that makes it harder for your opponent to return the shot.* Hmmm, I kept thinking. The whole point of a racquet sport is to make it harder for the opponent to return the shot. He didn't sell me, I sold myself! I bought the more expensive racquet having rationalized that I had made the right choice.

Let's break this down and apply it to your answer. Begin with the number of differences. In the sporting goods store, the seller's approach encouraged me to listen for ten differences. If later, someone asked me what the differences between the expensive racquet and cheaper alternatives, even if I forgot the details, I would have remembered there were ten differences. Had the seller not told me to listen for ten, I'd have heard a certain amount of statements and been unable to organize them in my head. Do you know what we do when we can't organize in our head the words we are hearing? We tune out.

And now list your differences. It doesn't matter how many, there are no magic numbers. But label each one by the number and a one-word label and then explain. So, your answer might sound like this: "number 1, flexibility. We are able to … (insert how you are flexible); number 2, scalable. We are (insert how your solution is scalable)." Again, the label for each difference increases the ability for the other person to remember and repeat your answer.

Now the hard part — thinking of the complete list of differences. You can easily come up with this list if you include the three kinds of differences you can possibly have.

> *The Takeaway: Make your answer repeatable by numbering and labeling every difference. But don't try to persuade; it's the absence of obvious persuasion techniques that makes the customer think favorably about your differences.*

List all three kinds of differences

Now you are wondering if you really have enough differences. It's best to pool a lot of people's answers when developing the "perfect" list of differences. In my workshops, I have taken companies through brainstorming exercises in small groups. In this way, we were able to get each group to identify a different set of differences.

Each group found it easier to find a lot of differences when instructed to look for these three kinds of differences:

- "USPs." The most literal kind of difference you can have versus your competitors are Unique Selling Points. Perhaps you are the only company with a certain ability or resource? In today's world, unique differences quickly become commodities. Which is why you also need:

- "By Degree" differences. From a high-level perspective, many competitors are similar. For example, almost every company has some kind of Customer Service. But perhaps your Customer Service speaks more languages, has more operational experience or formerly worked in the customer's business. These are subtle but important differences that are often overlooked which might be especially valuable to customers.

• "Solution Set" differences. Large companies have "umbrella services" providing many services under one roof. Small companies have fewer services but are "specialists." They criticize their larger "generalist" competitors. But the larger company boasts of the convenience of one point of contact and packaged pricing. Which solution are you trying to communicate: specialty or convenience?

The Takeaway: The customer will view you differently depending on the ways you are different from your competitors. Everyone's solution sounds the same, until you hear the details of the differences.

Developing and Perfecting Your Answer To: What Makes You Different?

Whenever you brainstorm anything at work, there is a tendency to become exhausted quickly and settle for an idea before the meeting ends. You end up choking off the remainder of your creative energy in your haste to tie up the loose ends into a finished, polished product before the hour-long meeting concludes. My advice is always to make brainstorming into two meetings. Don't let yourself even attempt to write the polished answer until you have brainstormed the list twice.

When you return to complete the brainstorming, you will see that your mind unconsciously will have grouped the answers. At the conclusion of your first brainstorming session, you had a disparate list of differences. Days later, when you revisit that list, you realize that you have three, four or five categories of differences. You name each category, for example: "technology differences," "service differences," "commercial differences."

Use those names in your script. For example:

"There are three differences. The first is Technology. We have the only...the second is service. Our dedicated service team will … the third is our commercial agreements. Our contracts allow customers to … "

You can always add multiple technology differences. But, by starting with a label, you don't have to worry about overwhelming the customer with too much information to follow and remember.

> *The Takeaway: By naming your differences, the customer will have another hook to remember them.*

Performance Tips: Change the Number Of Differences To Suit

When you ask, "Would it help if I told you how we are different?" you can expect a yes answer and an eager listener. Now you have their attention. They are not necessarily listening for a specific number but they are listening for real differences. So, you want to think: prioritize and personalize. By that, I mean you should make sure you only mention the differences most relevant to that customer. And deliver the list of differences in the order of impact. So, if your most important difference is Speed of Delivery, say it first. Don't assume you should save it for the last so you can make a big finish — you will have lost them by the time you get to it. And, if the only difference that matters to that person is Speed of Delivery, then customize the list for them by saying "there is one big difference between us and our competition … "

> *The Takeaway: There is no magic number of differences. Only choose to deliver the differences that matter most. To do that, you will need a longer list of differences from which you always choose the "greatest hits" most relevant to that customer.*

Question #3 – What is the advantage of working with you?

This is the information the customer is really interested in learning but only if we answer the question correctly. To do that, let's remind ourselves of the unasked questions behind this big question:

- *Why would a customer, like me, work with you?* (The understood but unmentioned part of this question: *I don't expect the seller to see the world the way my professional peers see our world.*)
- *When I tell a co-worker why I am interested in learning more about you, I need a story I can share that will inspire them too.*

In other words, the customer is inviting us to give them examples of success stories we've had with similar customers. They are not asking us to restate how we are different nor are they truly asking us for our opinion.

> **The Takeaway: When the customer asks us about our advantages, we have an opportunity to build credibility with success stories or turn off the customer with an overly "salesy" answer. Remember: Your job is not to shove your sale down the customer's throat. The seller's job is to help the customer decide what to do by giving them the information they need to make up their own mind.**

Knowing What to Say in Advance Will Help You Sound Great "In The Heat Of The Moment."

When I work with clients to craft the best answer to "What is the Advantage of Working with You?" (aka, What Makes You Better?) the usual problem is that the salespeople want to use the same answer for Differences and Advantages. As stated, the differences should sound like a helpful list of things that distinguish one brand, service or product from another.

But when the customer asks about the advantages, they are really asking "Why would I, that is a customer like me, with my job and my goals find *you* (that is, your company, product or service) better /advantageous? They are specifically <u>not</u> asking "Why would you, a salesperson who is paid to sell your service, think it's advantageous for me to buy?"

The customer is looking for proof. The biggest proof your services work is that others are buying from you.

Let me give you an example. Years ago, I ran a sales team that sold advertising inventory on an online media network. I was always looking to teach my team by my own example, especially when we were confronted with a difficult objection raised by an aggressive customer. For that reason, I joined many of our sales calls so my team could hear me handle the hardest questions and objections.

My company was the 10th biggest network, but we offered unique targeting and advertising opportunities on each of these sites. I had a memorable conversation with a media buyer who represented some of the biggest advertisers.

I was ready for their question, which came at me sounding more like an attack than a concern. Like a character in a movie, in the heat of the moment, I came up with a great line.

Media Buyer: You are a relatively small network. Why should I buy from you?

Me: I talk to a lot of media buyers. The media buyers who represent the top ten direct-response advertisers tell me that we are their best performing ad network.

> *The Takeaway: Once you have all of your lines down, you can make them sound like you just thought of saying them in a very natural sounding, unrehearsed way. You may or may not come up with a great line when you are using your improv skills. The more reliable way to consistently have a good sales conversation is to walk into each conversation already knowing your lines.*

Four Benefits to Knowing Your Advantages

After my team heard me use a new line, I'd bring them together for a "teaching moment." In this case, I asked them to consider psychology, both mine and the customers, by drawing their attention to these four things about my response:

- I avoided saying "well, I think we are the best network because I think / believe … " or "well, I think the advantage of working with us is … " I knew to avoid those phrases because I didn't want to trigger off this reaction: "who cares what you think? You are the salesperson, not a media buyer. Of course you think there is an advantage in working with your company! You are paid to say there is an advantage in working with you." And, they would have been right in thinking that.

- Because I knew that I could solve for presumably the worst-case-scenario objection, I was confident enough to call any buyer, even (especially?) the ones who I suspected would give me that objection.

- I was able to deliver a response to the buyer's attack without sounding defensive.

- I not only satisfied the concerns of the customer, I gave them a way to echo my pitch to their circle, even if their circle was skeptical.

> **The Takeaway: Your success stories are "people proof" that your service is right for similar customers. So, you need to know at least one story for each kind of customer you are selling to as well as know how to tell each story for the maximum advantage.**

Stories For All Occasions (You'll Need At Least Ten)

If you find yourself in a sales meeting talking to a small company and you bring up a success story about your experience working with an established global company, your story will backfire on you. The reverse is also true; a global company won't care that your solution worked for a much smaller company.

For that reason, you need a reassuring story for every kind of customer you sell to, including big customers, small customers, customers who also use your competitors but prefer your service, companies that have only ever used your company, etc.

If you are new to sales or are a recently hired salesperson, you don't yet have any of your own stories. In that case, you will need to learn stories from more experienced people at your company. Account Managers often have plenty of stories to share. Customer Success Managers and even Operations Managers can often supply even better stories because they work so closely with clients.

If there is no one else to turn to, you will have to go directly to the source — ask the customer. You may be surprised by what you learn.

Let me give you an example of the surprising stories you will hear. When I first got into training, I was with a company that only had one training program, a full-day workshop called Cold Calling (for those who got into sales during this century, you may have never heard of this — it's how to use the phone to make appointments with total strangers). At the time, I was a salesperson, not yet a trainer.

During the lunch break of this one-day program, knowing that there really was nothing to lose because there was no other sale to be gained from this client, I dared to ask the question that most sellers are afraid to ask. I asked the decision maker why he bought.

I expected him to tell me about his goal of improving his team's cold calling skills. I thought he might talk about the confidence gained from this kind of training. Instead, he surprised me with this answer. He looked at me and said "when you were selling me this program I could see how enthusiastic you were about your service. I was hoping that if we bought your training, our team would become as enthusiastic about our service as you are about yours!"

What? My enthusiasm was the thing he liked? Not the program itself? Not new skills? Who knew?

Over the years, I have learned to always directly ask customers why they buy. Not only do I learn surprising answers but the way they deliver their answers provides me with the best success stories.

> *The Takeaway: Assume you will need about ten stories to get through a typical work year. Over time, you will tell the same stories to many different people. Resist the urge to shorten the stories. Instead, focus on the human feelings, like **frustration** over challenges and **satisfaction** when your solution works.*

What Makes a Story Interesting Enough To Influence Your Customer And Their Circle?

The best stories become impactful when they are told so well the customer is moved to repeat them to their circle. To get your stories to that point you need to begin with brainstorming. Then capture the best ideas and mold them into a script. And then role play practice. Warning: scripting stories is harder than scripting "differences."

Learn to use your use-case, success stories and case studies as the foundation of your answer to "What is the Advantage of working with you?" But, to get the most mileage from your stories you need to know how to tell them.

Simply saying: "oh, we have lots of clients with that problem/challenge/ goal" is not story telling. Even worse is replacing the summary version with this line: "here is a one-page case-study of how we have solved this problem for others."

A well-told story is interesting enough to do two things: hold the listener's attention and enable them to repeat the highlights of the story to others.

To get there, your story should have these elements:

- <u>People</u>: A description of the characters described clearly enough for the listener to "see" themselves as one of the characters. In sales stories, your characters not only have corporate objectives, but they are also challenged by new problems and perhaps frustrated that their usual "in-house" solutions aren't working or haven't worked in the past.

- <u>Conflict</u>: Describing the customer's struggle makes the story sound more real. What were the characters trying to do? Explaining the character's motivation to solve a problem and do so in the right time and at the right budget can draw in the listener.

- <u>Resolution</u>: Not only what finally worked, but how much better the customer felt after finally solving the problem.

The Takeaway: To get better at telling stories you have to hear enough people telling stories that you can begin to understand the magic (unexplained process) of great story telling. My advice: Read more. Listen to podcasts. Watch documentaries.

Practice Telling Your Story by Telling the Punchline First

When we discussed role playing your answers to the "What do you Sell" and "What Makes you Different," the role playing, in part, helped you memorize the answer. But, when you practice using a story to answer "What is the Advantage of Working with you," focus on getting the right reaction. Often, the secret lies in telling the story in the right order.

For the most part, when we are trying to describe "work-stuff" to people outside of our own company, we aim for straight line explanations. First A, then B, then C and finally D. In that example, D is the conclusion, which I also call the punchline. Stand-up comics get a laugh when D is an unexpected punchline based on the A-B-C "set-up." But, unless you are going for a laugh, and the listener is listening for a punchline, you should begin with the punchline.

Why? Because the moment you launch into any story, the listener begins to mentally anticipate where you are going; what you are going to say. While they are anticipating, they are listening to see if they are right. Since they really don't yet know what to listen for, they may miss the part you want them to hear. To avoid this natural psychology, begin with the end.

For example, here is the template of a typical business story told A>D.

"We have a customer who can be described as ___. They had this problem: ____. We then approached them a year ago. We showed them ___. At first, they weren't sure, but eventually fell in love with us after they saw how we can help them.

Here is the same story, with the punchline first: "We have a client who loves us because of our solution. They were struggling with their challenge for a year and were sure nothing and no one could help them. Then, we showed them ___. They were like you — skeptical. But, over the course of our first year together, they learned _____."

When you begin with a punchline, the customer now knows where you are going with your story and primed to listen for the missing part: how you got there.

By correctly positioning the punchline, they will view the rest of your story through the right lens.

> *The Takeaway: Just because you are telling a story that proves how advantageous your company is, remember that people are always tuning out. Telling the story right keeps them engaged the whole time. And, by featuring the punchline in the beginning, they will definitely hear the most important part - the part you want you them to Echo to others.*

What Makes You Worth the Money?

Before we begin calculating numbers let's consider the psychology behind a reassuring answer.

First, let's consider the unasked questions behind this question.

- *How do I make more money than I spend by buying from you?*
- *If I have to defend the budget to someone else, what can I tell them?*

The B2B customer is often responsible for sourcing a solution for their organization. When they have finally decided what they want to do and who they want to do it with, they now have to defend their decision to a financial decision maker. That person isn't only wondering why a service is worth the money. They are calculating opportunity costs (what else they could do with the same money).

Think of the conversation between your customer and their financial decision maker when developing your answer to this important question.

> *The Takeaway: We need to help our customer successfully echo our ROI answer when they are talking to their financial decision maker.*

How Did You Buy a Similar Service The Last Time? (Word Choice)

The right answer to "how are you worth the money?" inspires the customer to echo the seller. The wrong answer makes the seller look pushy. Let me explain.

Everything in sales, including how you answer questions, is about relationship building. To build your relationship right, let's begin choosing the right words for our answer to "What makes you (your service) worth the money?" by using the answer to the question most salespeople fail to ask. Sellers should always ask how prospects have bought similar services in the past. Instead, they ask "how do you — or how will you - make decisions?" The well-intentioned salesperson who is looking to learn the prospect's buying process will get an aspirational answer when they ask about the future. But, customers, B2B or consumers, follow patterns. For that reason, the most likely buying process going forward is the one they used in the past. If a salesperson isn't asking about how — and why — decisions were made — and the cost justified - in the past, they can't really know for sure what to expect in the future.

If you answer right, the customer will echo your words to their circle with confidence. How do you do it right? By incorporating into your answer the prospect's past buying rationale.

My favorite example of this is when I visit a car dealership. I drive my own car to the dealer. The car salesperson should begin our conversation by asking about *that* car. Imagine how much they would learn about how I like to buy — and therefore how to sell to me — if they asked:

"What car are you currently driving? Why did you pick that car? How did you choose that model, those options, the dealership? Did you purchase? If yes, in cash or loan? Or did you lease?"

If they began the conversation there, they'd get me to reveal my past buying patterns. They'd learn how I like to buy cars. They might learn, for example, that the last time I spent more than three months looking. Or I bought the first car I saw on the first day I began looking. Or I never go into a dealer until I am ready to buy. Or I never buy from the first dealer I walk into on my first day of car shopping. Then they could ask how long I've been looking for a new car. Suppose I said today is the first day of my search. If they already knew how I buy, then they'd fit their sales process into my preferred way — and therefore wouldn't appear pushy.

But most car salespeople (not all of them, there a few good ones out there — and they get my repeat business) assume that I want someone to talk me into buying their car today. To me, it's like a game show — How Fast Can We Talk the Next Customer into Buying A $25k - $50k Car? Extra points for getting the sale completed in under 10 minutes. They want to push me into following *their* pattern. That's why customers like me think of them as pushy.

I mention this because ROI is in the mind of the customer. There are many potential ways to describe the value of your service — saves time, money, etc. There isn't only one way to do the "ROI math." Each customer has their own way of determining what is worth the price / cost and what isn't. The customer's way makes sense to them, which is why they follow their preferred pattern. The danger of using *your* (the seller's) ROI math rather than the customer's "historic" ROI math when buying similar services is that your argument will fall flat and they will think of you as pushy rather than worth the money.

> *The Takeaway: To give a memorable and echo-able answer to the question "what makes you worth the investment?" learn how your existing customers calculate ROI. Use "customer-centric ROI math."*

To Develop the Right Script, Think like an investor

To prepare to answer "What Makes you (your offering) Worth the Money," think like an investor rather than an employee.

As an employee, I see my company's current abilities based on our current resources. I see the market, that is, the "demands" of customers. I see the gap — what could we do if we only had other resources? How many more customers would be attracted to us if only we had a less expensive service, a more comprehensive service, an updated/improved service, an additional service. For this reason, employees can always imagine how a company could make more money if only someone poured in more investment (other people's money).

But, as an investor, I want a 2x — 100x return on every dollar (or other currency) I invest, as soon as possible. Even if I am willing to invest a billion, I will only incrementally invest that money a little at a time as a company proves itself worthy by reaching benchmarks after a minimum investment is made.

Spending money to make money is an often-quoted business expression. Employees think spending money always is the first step. Investors think spending money only leads to making money when 100 other things are in place first. The first way they see to make money: reduce expenses.

I mention this because the normal, risk-tolerant salesperson argument to customers is "if you buy my capabilities, you will make more money than you spend." But, when the salesperson begins to think like an investor, they change their argument to "your current investment only buys resources with limited returns. By redeploying some of your investment with my company, I can make your remaining resources more productive."

For example, if I sell a technology that enables customers to do certain tasks more easily, it is a mistake to argue — "buy my technology to reduce your work/effort/time." Even though that argument sounds right, the customer counters that argument with this one - "maybe your technology speeds things up, but it also introduces a new cost. Without that extra cost, my current resources are a pretty good deal — I get a nice return from my current resources."

It is much more persuasive to argue — "our technology will free up your current resources so they can now also do..." Now, the cost of your service is compared to the extra value of the additional services your technology enables.

To make this argument work, the seller must first demonstrate an understanding of the value of the work of the customer's resources. With that understanding, the seller can personalize their ROI argument to each customer. Personalized messages are more likely to echo between co-workers.

The Takeaway: Base your ROI argument on the value of the customer's current resources. It gives your decision-maker enough confidence to Echo Sell your service to their circle.

Practicing The ROI *Argument*: Don't Try to Beat Someone at A Game They Play Better Than You

Test your ROI argument with "friends" who know money better than you.

Let me give you an example. Years ago, I was working with a client in the B2B office product space. Public companies can spend so much on office supplies that if they could reduce those costs, they'd actually change their share price. While compelling, the argument will be challenged by people like CFOs (Chief Financial Officers) who study this topic all day long. Even though the sellers I was working with were very smart, and great presenters, I knew they thought like salespeople and not CFOs.

For that reason, I included their CFO, the FD (Financial Director) and others from their finance department into the training. I had the salespeople role play with their own employees who think like accountants, not like salespeople, or procurement people or decision makers who use the office products.

In each role play, the "customer" would instinctively challenge the salesperson. Not because the seller had a hole in their story, but because that is how money people think. Challenging everyone else who claims to know about money as well as they do produces this "knee-jerk" reaction to question every assumption. The first thing that happened in each role play was that the customer would pose a challenging question that the seller was unprepared to answer. Luckily, this was only a role play and those customers were actually friendly employees.

That tough practice produced confidence. The office products sales team I trained crushed their goals. And they shortened the sales cycles for their biggest sales. Rather than the usual "go to procurement and get your head handed to you" approach to selling office products, they went directly to the CFO of some of the biggest companies in the US. Once they won over that person, the internal Echo Selling began. The seller's pitch, repeated by the CFO, was more effective than the seller's pitch delivered directly to the procurement team and everyone else in the usual office products buying process.

> *The Takeaway: Role playing with the right people builds confidence, develops the optimal word choice and gets the right people to Echo your sale. Getting the right people to Echo your sales pitch works even better than the seller delivering the same pitch to everyone.*

Question #5 – Why Should I Buy from You? - Preparing To Deliver Your Point of View (POV)

Let's first unpack this question, before we explore the psychology, word choice and performance tips. For the moment, let's assume the customer literally asks you this question in the first meeting. (We'll see in a moment that it's not only their question you are preparing for; it's yours).

When imagining the customer asking, you can almost hear the "challenging" tone behind their question. For your answer to be right, it needs to reassure the person who would challenge the seller in this way, presumably in the first meeting.

For us to accomplish this, we need to remind ourselves of the questions behind the question:

- *You (the salesperson) know your own company and presumably know us. Given all of that insight, what is the logic behind your thinking that we should work together?*

- *Can you give me something I can use to explain to my circle (boss, team, peers) why they should consider buying from you?*

Remember: even if they don't ask, they are surely wondering. And you may be too.

Nothing helps your confidence more than being able to walk into each meeting prepared to answer their questions — as well as the question in your own head about why you are right for them.

> *The Takeaway: The answer to this challenging question, the hardest of the five to prepare for, is your point of view. You are not ready to talk to this customer until you can deliver this answer with confidence.*

Developing Enough Confidence for Your POV

If you watch salespeople pick the next lead on today's lead list, you will observe something unexplainable. Very few people will call every name on their own list. Each of us, governed by our own personal navigation system, will mysteriously skip over some leads and get attracted to others.

Salespeople, myself included, get a feeling about every lead on our list that only we understand. We look at some leads and think "I don't know about this one." (we skip over that one). Other leads make us say to ourselves "I don't think I'm ready for this one; I should wait." (We skip over that one, too, but promise ourselves to revisit it possibly in a few weeks or months when we are ready.) Some of the leads make us imagine the customer's unhappy expression upon hearing from us "I bet if I call them, they'll tell me they're not interested." But a few leads get us excited enough in advance to say to ourselves "I can't wait to talk to these people. We are exactly right for them. They should buy from us because..."

When we get that feeling about a lead before we contact them, we end up having our best sales conversation with them.

I have observed this common feeling in myself. It's for that reason, I prepare for first meetings by generating all of the reasons they should buy from me in advance of my call and especially in advance of my first conversation with them. That pre-thinking will enable me to have my best sales conversation. I often take a walk prior to important first meetings, reviewing in my mind all of the reasons I think the customer will like us and why I think we are right for them. By the time I begin talking to them, I not only have an answer to the question I imagine them wondering about ("What makes you think you are right for us?"), I have a well thought out point of view on the subject. Do you ever talk to someone with a strong point of view? Even if they were quiet up to that point, when that topic comes up, they become like a public speaker in front of a large audience, ready to deliver their speech. They are enthusiastic. Enthusiasm is contagious. Pass it on!

> *The Takeaway: Salespeople do things only we under-stand. Leverage the mysterious gravitational force that attracts us to some leads by preparing to deliver your point of view on the topic of why you are right for that customer. Prepare to discuss this with your prospect in the most enthusiastic and compelling way.*

Why should they buy from me? Let me count the ways

There are three steps I follow when I develop a POV statement.

Step 1 — imagine the look I want to see on the customer's face when I deliver my answer. That reminds me of the target. It's like plugging in the destination into your GPS; it keeps me focused.

Step 2 - answer this series of questions: ○

- What connects your company (your solution, product or service) to the customer's strategic mission?
- What connects your customer, personally, to your service?
- What is your ROI approach to helping similar clients?
- How do you help customers become more effective and efficient?
- What is the potential value of the opportunity gained if they work with you?
- What is the potential value of their loss by not working together?
- How would your service give the customer a competitive edge?

(In your attempt to answer these questions you will quickly learn what you don't know or can't answer. Use that insight to inform your pre-meeting research).

Step 3 - role play. In my case, I walk around the block talking out loud to myself. In the old days, you would get funny looks. But, if you hold your phone in your hand while walking, people will just assume you are talking to someone on the phone. ⌃⌃

> *The Takeaway: By following my questions, you will always have a starting point when brainstorming a great POV.*

Confidence Is Contagious; Confidently Delivering Your POV Is the Highest Form of Empathy

Remember, you are performing, not merely answering "Why should I buy from you?"

Let's start with this concept: People respond in kind to each other. If you begin with a smile, the other person will usually match you. If you say "hey, how are you?" The other person will ask how you are.

Customers feel less confident when they ask a salesperson for their recommendation and the salesperson seems unsure. Customers feel more confident when the salesperson answers with confidence.

You can try to fake confidence, but that only produces a "faked" reaction. But, genuine confidence, which comes from really understanding the customer's situation and goals, is unmistakable.

Bringing confidence to a customer who is deciding whether or not your solution is relevant to their needs requires the highest form of empathy. Consider that many people confuse empathy with sympathy. When I react to a confused person with patience and understanding I am sympathetic to their weakened state. But, when I show that person the light they are seeking, I am helping them in the way they want to be helped.

With that in mind, practice saying your POV until you feel the power of your conviction. This answer, unlike the other four we have discussed, "works" when the other person shares your confidence and enthusiasm. Don't simply think of answering a possible customer question. Instead, think of your POV as the answer to your own question: Why do I think I can help this person?

> **The Takeaway: Echo Sellers think about how confident they sound during pre-meeting preparation.**

Now that you have the "magic words" you are half-way there

Let's review how we got to this point and what we will cover next:

Part 1 — Understanding the Echo. This part defined Echo Selling and explained where Echo Selling fits into the universe of business communication.

Part 2 — Change Your Thinking Before You Can Change Others. This part explained how you must think differently in order to make Echo Selling work for you.

Part 3 — Echo Selling Word Choice & Performance Tips. This part explained what to say and how to say it.

Part 4 — Echo Selling Campaign Tactics. Now that you understand what Echo Selling is, how to think and what to say, you are ready to begin an Echo Selling campaign.

> *The Takeaway: Reading, thinking about and doing the assignments described in the first three parts of the book have prepared you to execute a successful echo selling campaign.*

PART 4
Echo Selling Campaign Strategy & Tactics

Advancing toward your goal one campaign at a time

Now that we have covered Parts 1, 2 & 3, you are ready to launch into Echo Selling. Like all worthwhile missions, Echo Selling can be the kind of goal we all have that we never really act on. I want to ensure you succeed! To get you there, we're going to follow four proven principles:

- Start small (*we're going to begin with a mini "campaign"*)
- Begin with measurable campaign goals. (*classic 'goal achieving' advice!*)
- Follow a strategy that plays to your strengths (*"leverage your laziness"*)
- Learn to use all of your tactics like levers. (*It's not finding the one lever "that works." It's the "level" of all of the levers*)

A good starting point is to launch a campaign aimed at three similar companies, for example, from one sector of your territory or one product line or vertical.

That's your opening Echo Selling lead list. One campaign, aimed at all three, will tell you exactly what you need to do to optimize and scale your Echo Selling going forward.

It's best to think of actual targets as we go through the strategies and tactics together. It's also ok to change your lead list as well as your measurable campaign goals as you read on.

To increase the odds of success and reduce the chance of failure, you need to follow a strategy and learn a set of effective tactics. To help you develop the right strategy, I will provide you with a "light" strategy framework. Then I'll cover the tactics you'll need to get there.

> **The Takeaway: Begin Echo Selling by targeting three similar prospects. Choose from the same industry. Customize your Strategy and Tactics, based on the framework I'll be providing in the next few chapters.**

Strategy, Messaging, Targeting & Timing

You begin Echo Selling by launching a campaign. When things go wrong, upon reflection, we often see the problem was we got off on the wrong foot. To make sure our first step into Echo Selling is right, let's be clear about the meaning of a Campaign.

A campaign is when you reach out to the market to get your intended target(s) to take desired actions.

An Echo Selling campaign is when you reach the target and their circle of influencers and get them to:

- Be aware of you / your company / your relevant solution (*for example, they recognize your name*)

- Associate your solution with their current and anticipated challenges (*for example, they say "funny, I just heard about your company."*)

- Find positive qualities about you / your company / your solution (*for example, they like that you share helpful content and/or they agree with your point of view*)

- Consider learning more about your / your company / your relevant solution (*for example, go to your website, follow your social posts, listen to your podcasts, etc.*)

What is your Echo Selling campaign strategy? To combine messaging, targeting and timing in a way that encourages customers to take those actions and become Brand Ambassadors.

What's your messaging? We'll adapt what we discussed in Part 3 to each platform. We'll differentiate your Email messaging from your InMail messaging in the Tactics section, which follows the Strategy section of this book.

What is targeting? For most salespeople, the pre-occupation with only reaching the "real" decision maker makes the target smaller and harder to hit. You will more likely hit the target if you are aiming for a bigger target (targeting more than one person). From an Echo Selling perspective, half the target is the so-called decision maker; that is, the one person in a position to push your sale through — as long as they get the internal support they need. The other half of the target is the broad range of people who are in a position to potentially influence your customer.

You will more likely hit more targets when you define the target more precisely. To simplify this process, we'll apply an *Echo Selling label* to the customer's current job title, so we know where to aim our Echo Selling activities, which I will review with you in the next few chapters.

Timing? In the context of prospecting and personal marketing, timing is usually described as a "cadence." For example, reaching out to the company owner once a month versus reaching out to a manager whose job is closely aligned with your solution once per week for four weeks.

But, for Echo Selling, the ideal timing is to reach everyone at the same time. You are trying to reach everyone before they see each other in an upcoming meeting. You will see why in the next few chapters.

> ***The Takeaway: Think of Echo Selling like you would an Advertising or Public Relations campaign. Your strategy is to convert people into Brand Ambassadors. Your messaging, targeting and timing will create conversations between your target and their influencers about you and your solution. This will encourage them to move forward with you.***

Timing and Targeting part A: Reach Both Halves of Your Target at Meetings

Consider how much time your customer spends in meetings. For most business roles, "the buyer's" quality time is spent in three kinds of meetings (and, in some cases, four):

1. Meetings with their boss
2. Meetings with their peers
3. Meetings with their own team.
4. Some have a fourth kind of meeting: a special committee / group (sometimes cross-functional / inter-departmental team) who are working together on a new project.

Begin building your "circle of influencer" database with the people attending your customer's most important meetings. They are currently influencing your customer. Their opinions matter to your customer.

These three or four meetings are important enough to be recurring on everyone's calendar: when other things don't happen, these meetings still happen.

Each meeting follows its own agenda which is often circulated in advance (sometimes for political reasons, details of the upcoming meeting agenda are shared with others who will not attend). These meetings are often followed by reports, also shared with people unable to attend.

From an Echo Selling perspective, that means that there are three kinds of meeting communication: Pre (agenda), Post (reports) and During (the meeting conversation, which is similar but not the same for meetings which are In-Person, Virtual "face2face" or "voice2voice"). Even though you are aiming for meeting attendees, your message will reach the others whose influence is so strong they don't even have to attend the meeting to receive meeting communication.

Talk about a lot of meetings and communication about those meetings! Your decision maker and the other meeting attendees engage during 3 or 4 weekly/monthly meetings and receive 3 communication "opportunities" per meeting. That's 9-12 meeting communication opportunities (written and verbal) each month involving your customer and a potential list of influencers. Each "opportunity" reminds meeting attendees to think about their goals, identify challenges, create a list of actions, rearrange priorities, update forecasts and issue progress reports.

As a result, meeting attendees think about problems and solutions, challenges and resources, needs and next actions 9 — 12 times a month.

Psychologically, meetings and pre and post communication provide the right context to make a salesperson's related pitch seem relevant. As you will recall from our earlier conversation about digital thinking, particularly digital marketing, relevance is what turns unseen background *white noise* into something you notice.

> **The Takeaway: Meetings and their surrounding communication provide 9-12 times each month for buyers to think about their challenges and possible solutions. The most important 3 or 4 meetings are the perfect "trigger points" for your Echo Selling. Begin Echo Selling by targeting all of those meeting attendees.**

Timing And Targeting Part B: Reach People Just Before the Meeting

What's your goal of reaching them in time with the right message? Of course, devoting an entire meeting to discuss buying your solution is a great goal and a possible opportunity. But the more common scenario is your name comes up because they were discussing their problems/challenges/limitations which your solution addresses. And, the discussion occurred during your Echo Selling campaign which caused them to think of you, just in time, when the topic came up in their meeting.

It's not only that people will be talking together at meetings. Some of the influencers at those meetings get enthusiastic about topics they care about the most. Enthusiasm is contagious. "Meeting talk" is the best environment for Echo Selling, if you can get them talking about you.

The targeting and timing will work, providing you craft the right message. Your messaging (what you say and the platform you say it on, i.e., emails, InMails and social posts) builds credibility about your solution and reassurance about your fit for their needs. To get your Circle of Influencers to view you in the best light, you must "personalize" your messaging based on their likely motivation and the direction their influence flows. To make that clearer, we'll apply an Echo Selling label to meeting attendees in the next chapter.

> *The Takeaway: The path that leads to Echo Buying, where the seller reaches every influencer, is through the 3 or 4 weekly / monthly meetings which brings decision makers together with influencers. Our Echo can enter customer thoughts and conversations during the 9 - 12 weekly/monthly "communication opportunities."*

Learn The Direction the Influence Is Flowing

The ZMOT — the zero moment of truth - when influencers can potentially influence your decision maker is when they talk together at meetings.

Let's simplify our understanding of individual motivation and political power by assigning an Echo Selling label to every meeting attendee. This way, we can determine who and how they are likely to influence. I suggest you think about your target prospects and customers as we apply a label to everyone's role.

Let's look at an example: Imagine you are a B2B Salesperson, selling to midsize and larger companies. You sell Research/Data (access to your database of facts and insights as well as custom market research projects). Every kind of company buys some information. Any company looking to grow buys more information from you or from one of your competitors.

Your main contact is usually the head-of-research, but they may have many titles. Their Echo Selling label is Commercial Manager. Often, Commercial Managers have your product in their title. For example, as a sales trainer, I often sell to the Head of Training; Communication/ Technology providers sell to the head of Communication /Technology.

In this case, your Commercial Manager is also your day-to-day contact. The person who has your product in their title is usually the right person to deal with starting year two. But, they're not always the *only* right person for year one.

The Commercial Manager's research team are the Super Users. Commercial Managers can also be a Super User or a former Super User or not even a registered or trained User, let alone a *Super* User.

Commercial Managers and their teams support other teams in their company. Sometimes, Commercial Managers specifically use the solution you sell them to service other teams or departments. We call those other teams/departments Internal Customers.

Sometimes the budget to buy your service is allocated (partly shared) by the Internal Customer. Internal Customers who are interested in acquiring more of your service can be motivated enough to be your Coach. A Coach is motivated to help themselves by helping you. They'll push to get more allocated funds pointed in your direction if they really benefit directly from your service … depending on how your service relates to their goals.

The key to getting the messaging right: learn (don't assume) everyone's role and goal. By the way, don't be surprised to learn everyone's goals are different, sometimes contradictory.

The Takeaway: Influencer roles include Super Users, Commercial Managers, Internal Customers and Coaches. Internal Customers and Coaches are often more motivated and better positioned to help you than Super Users. Regardless of their role, helping people achieve their goal is what motivates them to help you. Before you can help them, you need to learn their goals.

Use Echo Selling to Reduce the Risk of Cancellation

Echo Selling can save cancellations if you get to influencers early in the sales process.

Continuing our example, suppose this year, the Head of Research is thinking of saving money by cancelling their contract with you because only one department (an Internal Customer) uses your information.

If your relationship with the account is limited to this one "decision maker" Commercial Manager, you have no more moves left to save the sale. But, by using Echo Selling to get to influencers, we still have a chance to find a Coach who can help you.

Let's suppose the one department still requesting the information through the Research Department is the Head of Sales who thinks your subscription research enables their sales team to find better leads. That's a strong motivation for them to vote for supporting your research and against cancelling the subscription. Strongly motivated, well-positioned Internal Customers can be your best Coaches.

Consider corporate politics when trying to understand the flow of influence. For example, the Sales Department usually has more clout than the Research Department because Research is a cost center and Sales is the profit center. The Head of Sales can try to impact the Head of Research's decisions. They can and do use their influence - at the meetings they both attend - to change or redirect budget decisions that favor them.

Those meetings may have names like the "Production Meeting" or "Investment Meeting." But, from an Echo Selling label point of view, we'll call them Operations Meetings.

> *The Takeaway: Internal Customers have a motivation that is aligned with the salesperson who is selling the service they want. They both want the sale / access to the service. The best opportunity for Internal Customers to influence Commercial Managers is during Operations Meetings.*

Operations Meetings Bring Commercial Managers and Internal Customers Together

It is easy to visualize how influence works at team meetings and meetings with a boss. But Operations Meetings introduce unanticipated opportunities for Echo Sellers looking to connect the people who benefit from your service with the people who buy it.

Despite being famously boring, every company, big and small, has Operations Meetings daily, weekly or monthly. If organizations have one meeting, it's the Operations meeting.

Attendees include the Head of Sales, the Heads of (or important delegates from) Marketing, Production, Research, etc. Apart from discussing the agenda, it creates a weekly or monthly reason for these people to talk to each other.

What do they have to talk about? Officially, they meet to discuss matters that pertain to them all: resource allocation, support, operational progress, anticipated challenges, timelines and budgets. Unofficially, they use Operation Meetings to claim credit, avoid blame and point fingers.

Echo sellers can help meeting attendees mentally connect their solution to those standard meeting topics with the right messaging.

> *The Takeaway: Learn who sits with your Decision Maker in Operation meetings. "Fit into" their meeting agenda by aligning your benefits with their goals in your messaging.*

Goals by Roles

An increase in Internal Customer demand can lead to increased budgets from your buyer, the Commercial Manager, depending on how well aligned your service is with the Internal Customer's goals. The more the Internal Customer sees your service helping them achieve their goals, the more influence they will exert over your Commercial Manager.

Commercial Managers often have different - and sometimes opposite goals - from Internal Customers as well as their own team. For example, Commercial Managers complain their team is stretched too thin when Internal Customers want more. But, the Commercial Manager may make the opposite argument with their Boss ("oh sure boss, we can handle more!") versus their own team ("Guys — I was telling everyone how hard you are currently working - we can't take on any more without some additional resources!"). Showing how you can help a Commercial Manager may only take you so far. To get more demand, start helping the Internal Customer — by first learning their goals.

Bosses (especially Senior Management / Owners) are another group with goals that may be at odds or simply different than everyone else's.

For example, the owner may be looking for an exit strategy of selling the company in two years by making it more productive now.

Senior Management Coaches may want increased cooperation between the Commercial Manager and all of the Internal Customers — because they see the lack of cooperation between department heads as a *people problem* they need to address. They may see your service as a means to that end.

> **The Takeaway: Often the Commercial Manager is the "decision maker." But nothing drives increased sales more than increased demand from Internal Customers.**

How Super Users Influence Commercial Managers

Sellers have the easiest conversations with Super Users because they "get" your product / solution better than anyone else on the customer side. Sellers hope these "informed" users will convince their boss to buy (or buy more).

But the Super User's ability to help sellers get a sale, renewal or account growth may be limited. From a "right-message to the right-person at the right-time perspective," the things that help Super Users may be opposite from the things that help Commercial Managers.

For example, a common benefit to Super Users is "ease of use." But ease-of-use may be only marginally interesting to the Commercial Manager who is more concerned with the ROI of every expense in their budget.

The Commercial Manager may want more work done in less time. The Super User wants the right level of workload as well as the promise of ongoing work / ongoing employment. The Commercial manager may be more interested if your solution would increase everyone's effectiveness so much that the department could save money and have a smaller team. Or, a power-hungry Commercial Manager may want to take on more work than the current team can handle, as a justification for more power, increased budget, or expanded head-count. Meanwhile, the Super Users may enjoy more power in a smaller team (*big fish in a small pond*) and worried that their contribution may be diminished in a bigger team.

For that reason, spending sales time communicating with Users presents sellers with good news and bad news.

The good news: The Commercial Manager will likely discuss most ideas for new services that would impact the team's productivity and happiness during meetings with their team of Users and Super Users.

The bad news: Those Users may not have the political power or relationship with their boss to influence anyone to *make* a purchase (buy your service, for example). But they likely have the power to say NO (as in "no, that won't make me / us happy"). That may be all the negative reaction the Commercial Manager / Decision Maker needs to hear as justification to stop considering your sale.

> **The Takeaway: With the Super User's support alone, we can't get a sale but without their support your sale may be dead in the water.**

Campaigns Need a Good Strategy and Excellent Execution

My strategy framework for you is to begin with a campaign targeting three similar companies. With each company your strategy is to:

a. Identify the Commercial Manager, their team of users, the Internal Customers that the team supports and the *most- likely-to-be-motivated-to-help-us-help-them* Coaches.

b. Consider the relative political power of each person.

c. Anticipate who attends the three or four "likely" meetings the commercial manager attends with their influencers. Those meetings include Team meetings with Users, Boss meetings (with their boss, senior management and/or owner(s) and Operation Meetings with peers / potential Internal Customers.

d. Find opportunities to communicate with everyone so you can learn their goals.

e. Find Internal Customers who are (or will) experience success with your service.

f. Nurture all the relationships with potential Internal Customers that can develop into Coaches.

g. Learn to master all five tactics needed to reach all the right people with the right message just in time for their next meeting.

The Takeaway: Your strategy is to identify everyone by their "influencer" role so you can target them in advance of the next meeting they attend with your Commercial Manager "buyer."

Five Tactics to Reach the Right People

Ok, so we now have a Campaign Strategy: get to the right people, beginning with the right meeting attendees. How will you reach them? By mastering these Five Echo Selling campaign tactics:

(Caution: each tactic, like everything else - in this book and in life - is simple, but not easy)

a. Research - Research to determine who to target

b. Social Selling - Begin with Social Selling, which among other benefits, makes them more likely to read your emails

c. Email Marketing - Follow-up with Emails, to deliver your messaging

d. Testing - Test, which is the number one way to know what really works and to achieve improvement.

e. Tracking - Track your results, which encourages you to be your own cheerleader and coach

I recommend you mentally apply everything we say in this part of the book to a potentially large customer and a small customer. Echo selling will work for both, but you'll need to adjust for size.

The Takeaway: Execute your Echo Selling campaigns by mastering the five essential tactics described above.

Research To Find the Right People

The goal of your research is to learn who is in your customer's circle of influence.

We already know from a high level that we will begin by looking for attendees to the three or four most important meetings "your customer" regularly attends. Also look at the customer's past history (previous roles) and thought leaders they follow online and elsewhere when looking for influencers.

There are three ways to research to identify potential "right people" (aka, decision makers and influencers):

a. Technology

b. Your sales notes

c. Allies

We'll look at all three individually. Without spending enough time researching, you may miss some important influencers who can't be found any other way.

> *The Takeaway: As a seller, time is your most important resource. Spending enough time on the right activities is like maintaining a balanced portfolio of investments. Make sure you invest time doing research every week.*

Technology, Especially Linkedin, Is the Starting Point for Research

For most salespeople, buyers and influencers can be found on LinkedIn. Outside the US, depending on the industry, other social media platforms need to be considered as well.

There is no one platform for all needs because not every individual is listed or mentioned in any one platform. And, of course, people move jobs and are sometimes slow in updating their profile or have protected themselves behind a wall of security settings.

Technology and research platforms are always popping up, growing, acquiring others or merging with each other. Stay on top of the latest developments among technology and information providers, especially the industry specific providers.

Choosing the right platform is only part of the challenge of using social media for business. The bigger issue is understanding the mindset of the user when they are on social media versus when they are on another website. The digital term which describes that mindset is "relevance."

Content is not inherently relevant, but it is relevant when it is what the user is looking for — and expecting — at that moment. So, if the user is looking for weather information and finds it on a particular webpage, it is relevant, useful and interesting. The user is more likely to engage with relevant content. But, when the user is looking for something else — for example a how-to video - and they instead bump into weather information, that same information is now irrelevant — and considered unhelpful and therefore less likely to be engaged with or clicked on.

Digital marketers understand that users are driven by one of four intentions every time they are online: social intentions, purchase intentions, "information-entertainment" intentions and purchase intentions. Echo Sellers not only want to reach the most targets, they want to reach people when their target is open to hearing from them. The user on Linkedin is looking for — and open to — business related messages that meet their social, information and education intentions. That is why I say that Linkedin is right for most salespeople.

> *The Takeaway: Make research a standing appointment in your calendar. Assume LinkedIn will be your "go-to" technology for research but try to find industry specific tools and other lead-gen sources to get a complete picture of all of the individuals you need to reach. Researching about research tools is as important as anything else you do. Make sure you are on top of the latest trends and little known new "gems."*

Human Research Requires Interviewing, Not Selling Skills

Possibly the best example of human research is your notes.

Your notes can reveal important clues about the person you are selling to, how they fit into their organization and who they potentially influence. But your notes will merely describe what you told them unless you get the conversation flowing in the right direction by engaging your interview skills instead of your default "sales skills." Let me explain the difference:

When I engage my sales skills, I match each comment the prospect makes with a similar comment of my own. So, if the customer says they are trying to improve their productivity, my *sales skill reflex* is for me to shoot back with "that's great! We specialize in helping companies improve productivity. For example, there was this one company who was trying to become more productive and they found our solution was the only one … " (I exaggerated for effect, but you know what I mean.)

The instinct to match their topic with our own story is ingrained in many people (sales and non-sales alike). But, as soon as you go into your "matching story," you are changing the conversation flow.

Ironically, the moment we match them, we are not bonding with them, which is what attracts us to that conversation tactic in the first place. Instead, we are replacing their flow with ours.

When the customer was talking, it was the "all about them" show. Then, we practically cut them off to tell them our matching story, which stops their flow by turning the conversation into the "all about us" show. Don't let that happen in your conversations. Your interview skills are all about keeping the conversation all about them and resisting all urges to make it all about you.

When I abruptly redirect their flow, by selling me rather than interviewing them, I've made the customer feel less encouraged to share.

What do we want them to share? We need to ask everyone:

- Who do you report to? (Learn potential boss meeting attendees)

- Who reports to you? (Learn potential team meeting attendees)

- Who / which departments do you support? (Learn potential Operation Meeting attendees)

> *The Takeaway: During the research phase, encourage, don't stop, the customer's conversation flow. When we don't encourage people to talk, they say less. Remember you are trying to learn, not convince.*

Allies: The Competitive Edge for Research

Technology and your sales notes from every customer interaction will take you pretty far. But there is one more place to go for a competitive edge: Allies.

Allies are other salespeople who sell to the same people you do, but who don't directly compete against you. You can try to include direct competitors, too, and I encourage you to try, if you can avoid the obvious danger of giving away too many secrets. Salespeople see the world in a way that others don't. For that reason, I value their insight. But, the big insight, from a research perspective, is that allies often know a key piece of information about my customer or prospect which I did not know.

I have built my business through Allies that grew into partners. For example, a competitive salesperson and I met at a trade show. We stayed in touch and a few years later, when both of our jobs changed, we created an SEO consulting agency together.

A person you meet may have begun as an intern and is now running the department, division, company - or even their own company. At various points in your career, you may end up buying from each other, selling to each other, or hiring each other. Famously, the best outcome is that the two of you become friends outside of work, too.

> *The Takeaway: Reduce the risks associated with having no network when times are tough by building a network of allies whenever you have the opportunity.*

Identifying People by Their Role and Their Spot On The Organizational Chart

You may be asking yourself why do you need technology, your notes plus allies to complete your research? What are you trying to learn?

You need everyone's help to stay current about your customer's and prospect's landscape beginning with the "decision maker" plus everyone they report to and reports to them.

This is not the same as asking everyone "how do they make purchase decisions?" which, among other things, is a hard-to-answer question and a *conversation stopper*. I want them to answer an easy question: how do these people (the customer's employees and in some cases, consultants, owners and investors) relate to each other from an organizational chart point of view? When do they talk to each other?

Expect complication. Expect to learn "it was one way up until last month, but starting this month or next, things are changing … you'll read about it … "

Often, we see special-project, cross-functional teams, each with budget-allocation, decision-making ability, but all need to run the "actual" decision past someone else — either budget holders, C-level, owners or senior execs or procurement or a combination.

In other words, in the end, the sale happens when a lot of people say yes and just as important, none of the right people said no.

> **The Takeaway: All three forms of research are needed for you to learn everyone's role and how they fit together on the "org chart."**

Social Media DOs & DON'Ts: Would You Walk into A Cocktail Party to Sell The Host Insurance?

When I mention social media to salespeople, they tend to think of free messaging. When I mention to buyers how salespeople use social media, they think of SPAM.

No one starts off with a plan to create social media messaging that looks like SPAM, but we end up doing that when we don't follow these social media rules:

a. Originality is the most interesting quality. To achieve that, you need to consider what other messages your target is receiving.

b. Subscribe to newsletters and blogs to read social media experts in order to receive lists of phrases to use and avoid.

c. <u>Over-Balance Giving Value</u> - Every kind of communication, either on social media or email, can be divided into two piles — asking for money or giving value. Asking for a "quick demo" or a "five-minute conversation over coffee" (even when you are offering to pay for that coffee) is asking for money. Giving insight with no strings attached is giving value. Make sure you tip the balance toward giving value before asking for money.

d. <u>Don't sell</u> - to anyone before they ask for your sales pitch.

e. <u>Social Selling isn't only for sales on social media</u> — It's for introductions, too. Remember: It's not what you know, it's who knows you ... and, how you were introduced. Introductions originally made via social media lead to better phone and email response rates.

> **The Takeaway: just because you are in a hurry to create an appointment with prospects, don't rush into a sale with anyone on any platform. Patience and giving value will produce more sales conversations over time. Keep the social in social media by asking for – and offering - introductions.**

Synergistic Advertising

The salesperson's instinct is to try to discover the one thing that works.

Let me give an example: A friend of mine is an A seller. He's tireless in his prospecting and is like a movie detective when it comes to reaching decision makers. He's always finding a new strategy to close a deal and shares his secret with me when he finds a winning one. One day he called me to report his newest finding: a better performing subject line, which seemed to generate a higher response rate than any other email subject line he ever used. While I admired his creativity and enthusiasm, my knowledge of advertising made me skeptical about giving this new subject line all the credit.

In his view, the new subject line worked like the missing ingredient in a gourmet meal which finally made his email campaign work. Sellers often attribute success to one thing. I agree that the subject line may have been the "final straw" compelling reason which finally moved the prospect to engage. But, in my view, the more likely secret to his success was the combination of the optimized subject and the context.

The advertising term for context is "synergistic."

While he was right to test different subject lines, he may have been wrong in attributing all of the success to the one change. Why? Because of the synergy of messages that the user is surrounded by, which include:

- All of the other messages that seller has ever sent to that prospect and their company. So, if the "average" prospect responds to the 3rd email (or the 15th email) all of the previous emails that reached the prospect before they engaged all combined to form the context.

- Plus all of the InMails the seller has sent prior to the email with the great new subject line.

- Plus all of the competitor's emails during that period of time.

- Plus the combination of the articles, blogs, newsletters, podcasts (all of which are social media messages, by the way) plus advertisements and personal recommendations that the prospect engaged with during the email campaign which included the "magic email with the optimized subject line."

- Plus all of the marketplace changes that occurred during that same email campaign which acted like a trigger to cause the prospect to finally engage now.

- Just as certain, absent all of that synergy, the new subject line alone is unlikely to convince an otherwise disinterested prospect to finally respond to the email.

Classic synergistic advertising examples include TV ads that generate online traffic to Google's search engine. Radio ads increase people's attention to billboards. Catalogs mailed to people's homes increases web traffic to the catalog's website which in turn boosts online sales.

__The Takeaway: Synergistic Advertising is when one medium makes another medium work better.__

Writing Which Improves Results

We've talked a lot about what not to do with Social and Email messages. What is the right thing to do? The "safe play" when messaging prospects, customers, decision makers and influencers is to be simple, direct, conversational and enthusiastically optimistic.

By simple, I mean best word choice.

Direct means getting to the point in a professional and collegial manner.

Conversational means finding the right balance of friendly and formal, appropriate for your relationship.

Enthusiastically optimistic means that you show a real interest in everyone you meet in hopes of finding potentially mutually beneficial ideas that you both can act on. Your passion for solving problems is contagious if communicated correctly.

Notice what didn't make the list: long explanations of how your products, services, solutions work. Guesses and assumptions about what each customer is looking for right now. Links and attachments offered prior to building trust. In other words, don't do what most salespeople are doing with their email and social marketing.

> *The Takeaway: Always make your business email and social messages simple, direct, conversational and enthusiastically optimistic.*

Social Selling "Rules"

Social selling is purposeful selling. It is not mass reach with an expectation of 1-3% rate of return. The goal is to reach an *essential-to-our plan* contact and produce the right reaction.

For best results, remember that social selling must primarily follow social "rules." I am not only referring to the rules for each individual platform but the hard-wired social rules we all follow — and bristle at when others don't follow. The moment we violate those rules, they turn off all engagement. In my view, those social rules are best spotted at a party. Socially, we all prefer to connect, engage and then convert— in that order. For example, we feel uncomfortable when people try to engage with us before we've connected, or they try to "close" us (get us to take some action, aka "conversion") before we properly talk first.

Social rules are complicated, in part because the order of when you do things is the most important thing to get right. The next time you go to a social media site (or a party), remember to first Connect, then Engage. Convert, only after the right amount of engagement.

> **The Takeaway: Expect the other person on social media to remember their hard-wired social skills – and their expectations of others. They expect you to Connect before you Engage and chose the right engagement point before you attempt to Convert.**

Connect, Engage and Convert

I am focusing on LinkedIn, which is generally the best-choice platform for B2B sales as well as a good choice for *first-one-to-get-right* if you are using multiple social media platforms. I recommend that you use all of the platforms that you think are relevant. But, I warn you that from a time management perspective, coming up with enough content so you can update all the major platforms the right number of times per day and week can be exhausting. So, if you are phasing your way into social gradually, begin with LinkedIn.

When connecting on LinkedIn, you are provided a bonus message opportunity. I recommend you use it. Introduce yourself by explaining who you are, who you both know, and why you thought it would be mutually agreeable to connect.

There are no magic words. Test different approaches. Track all of the word choices you make so you can measure best performing connection requests. You will eventually learn that short, honest and sincere works best.

Once they connect, engage them with these six tactics all designed to generate engagements.

1. Post something, which they'll see because of the recency of your engagement.

Important note: Eventually you will have to grapple with the question "how often should I post?" Different experts will recommend different weekly frequency guidelines depending on your goals. Those experts won't really answer how you can find and create the recommended number given that social media isn't your only job. This expert provides these two-time management tips: first — only commit to the amount you can realistically and reliably produce and post each week. Don't sabotage your efforts by giving yourself too big a hurdle to jump over every week. Second — Get the most mileage from your first post / all your posts by timing them with your connecting to the specific individuals you are targeting for your Echo Selling campaign.

2. Add a like /comment to something they've posted. They will get a notification about your engaging with their profile/content, which is a prompt to check out your profile.

3. Give value, before you ask for money. Offer relevant information, insight, expert opinion, stats, graphs and info-graphs. Make sure it's relevant to them, not just you.

4. Offer to share something — Make people feel special by sharing a widget, gadget, invitation to a new community, or something the other person will consider valuable.

5. Offer to help- If appropriate, offer to connect them to a person they are trying to reach.

6. Ask for their opinion — When we ask another for their opinion we are honoring and respecting them. But make sure your question isn't a set-up for a sales pitch.

These six tactics will increase the odds they will engage with you. But, before they do, expect them to check out your profile. Therefore, optimize your profile before driving people to it by following my 4-step LinkedIn Profile optimization guide described in the next chapter.

The Takeaway: Fight the urge to start selling in your first contact. Follow these 6 tactics to get engagements. Remember to optimize your profile first.

Optimize Your Profile to Change How Others View You

All of your efforts to connect with people on LinkedIn will, first and foremost, drive traffic to check out your LinkedIn profile. The role of your profile is to make a great first impression. While experts will tell you a dozen or more possible things to change, my 4-step, quick-start approach will get you most of the way there in the shortest time:

1. You — in a nutshell: Make sure your description text is properly edited so that anyone who sees it gets the right message, which is *you are a helpful professional and not a sales-closing-machine.*

2. Update your act: Update your profile often, always changing anything that looks too much like other salespeople's profiles, especially your competitors. Updating sends a quick note to your connections that you are still out there. Optimizing (your profile and everything else you care about) is an ongoing activity. Nothing "*one & done*" ever keeps improving.

3. Make everyone feel welcome: When people consider whether or not to connect with you, they'll make their decision in part based on your profile and your connections. Make sure you already have some connections just like the people you are targeting (same industry, same specialty, same job title, etc.).

4. Rewrite history: Rewrite all of your jobs, not just your current one. Your job history should not appear as a resume or CV, but rather a story about you. That story is that your whole life so far has led you to this moment where you are in a position to bring your talents and passions to help others. If the reader sees a bunch of different jobs without the story line, the only story is that you move around a lot.

The Takeaway: Consider the story your target is picking up from your profile. Follow these 4 steps to ensure you shape their understanding of who you are and the value that you can potentially bring them.

Wait, Did I Forget to Mention Using The Phone?

Salespeople who don't believe in using the phone would agree. Phone-skilled salespeople would argue that using the phone would eliminate steps between targeting and talking to the person you are trying to reach.

Most sellers are better talkers than writers, which is a good reason to consider using the phone. By phone you can combine your personality, humor and questions in order to react in real time and pivot when needed. Obviously, you can't easily do any of that by email.

The greater your skills, the greater your confidence level in everything you do! Without the right phone skills, you won't have the confidence and will rationalize to yourself why phones don't work for sales.

More important than choosing between phone or email is the Big Picture Goal, which is to create a great first impression. We need others to echo their positive impression of us.

You can accomplish this goal by combining phone and email. If you call them before sending an email, your email may be a summary or confirmation about what you spoke about. It makes you look like an extremely helpful professional when you memorialize a phone conversation or meeting in a follow-up email. If your email precedes your call, then properly summarizing your reasons for reaching out can increase the reader's interest in engaging with you. The opposite is true, too: If the email is not properly written, it will not produce the right reaction and might even be totally ignored.

The lesson is: increase your confidence by improving both your phone and writing skills. With both skills, you will have more options and more ways to create a great first impression.

The Takeaway: The answer to "should I phone or email?" is phone if you have the skills and confidence; email if you don't have those skills. Phone AND email if you have the skills to do both, which will give you a competitive edge over the "email-only" or "phone-only" sellers who are competing with you for your target's attention.

Write For All the Readers, Not Only Your Intended Target

Emails serve two purposes — the first is to properly communicate your message to your intended target. The second is to properly communicate your message to others who see your emails when your intended target secretly forwards it to them. The best practice for Echo Sellers is to consider this "secret forwarding" whenever you send any digital content, whether it's an email or proposal. Make sure you keep your message short and personalized, but able to impress the others who receive a copy.

As an Echo Seller, I count on that secret forwarding. My thinking is that if I do trigger enough interest, my target (buyer, Commercial Manager, main point of contact, etc.) will share my note or document with the others in their world whose opinions they care about most. I believe the more compelling my email (and other documents), the more likely this sharing occurs. And, in case my research misses this "secret other person," secret forwarding solves the problem. But, only if I write my email for both readers.

How do I make each document right for both intended and secret readers? By always focusing on building credibility with a professional tone. So, even if you covered the "credibility stuff" (you and your company's capabilities and successful record of helping others), repeat that same information, even a shortened version, in every email and document.

My advice is for you to look at your emails, and all other digital assets you share, through the eyes of a stranger. Ask yourself will that other person, who only knows about you through this one email or document, think highly of you based on what you sent?

The Takeaway: Assume the person you send an email to will secretly share your note with an influencer in their life, whether or not they reply to your note. Always write emails and other documents, for both readers.

Four Email Gates – Are Yours Locked or Unlocked?

Sales emails have four parts, or gates.

When the gates are unlocked, you have created a path which guides the reader towards a conversation with you. While some readers, especially the ones that know and love you, will jump over locked gates, the rest will simply move onto the next email in their inbox if any gates are locked.

As a trainer, coach, manager, prospect and customer, I have analyzed thousands of emails and email drafts that salespeople have sent or intend to send. I see a few truly original email messages, where all the gates are unlocked. But mostly I see the same "locked-gate email templates" from thousands of different people. My advice is to put yourself in a position to see other salespeople's emails. How? By shopping for services and requesting information whenever you can. Salespeople will send you their templates. Compare their approach to yours. If they look alike, change your approach.

The good news and bad news is that 90% of salespeople's emails have locked gates. By unlocking your email gates, you can put your email ahead of the 90% of salespeople competing for your prospect's time and attention.

We'll examine each gate individually, but the common theme is the degree to which your messaging is helping the customer. When the only person being helped is the salesperson, the gates remain locked.

That sounds obvious when you are looking at another salesperson's emails. We need to be as good at spotting locked gates — by looking at who is being helped - when looking at our own emails.

Common examples of only helping yourself and ironically locking your own email gates include:

- You promise to share your advice — but only if they contact you (*I have a great idea I want to share with you.* Please *click below to conveniently schedule a meeting with me so I can tell you all about my idea*)

- You reach out by email to tell someone that you are running a sale / offering a discount (*but only if you act now*).

- You send an email intended to communicate that you are honest and sincere but use the same template that the bottom 90% of sellers send. Lack of originality in cold emails signals to the reader that you are not honest or sincere, a classic way to lock the gate to the reader's attention.

The burden on Echo Sellers is to find original messaging. Of course, it helps the lazy salesperson who skips the work of creating quality messaging by simply writing what everyone else writes. But when readers recognize the same template, they skip the work of considering anything you are trying to communicate.

In the following chapters, we will examine each of the four email gates individually. This will help you get better at spotting who, if anyone, is being helped at each gate.

> **The Takeaway: Email gates are locked when you are only helping yourself.**

Gate #1 - Does Your Subject Line Encourage or Stop Conversations?

Salespeople often get this one wrong and as a result, their emails go unopened. The busy person with a mountain of emails to go through is looking for an easy way to determine which ones they will open and which ones they will skip. The "subject line test" the reader will apply to your emails is whether or not they see something — or someone - they recognize.

For example, suppose you sell advertising services that benefit brands by improving their advertising results. You recently closed a deal with XYZ who bought because of that benefit. Now you are looking for your next sale and the next lead on your list is Chris Jones, the Ad Manager for the ABC brand.

Your email is sort of like an ad — it must capture the attention of the right person. So you consider the subject line that summarizes your benefit, for example:

Subject line: Improve your Ad Campaign Results

Subject line: Improve Your Next Campaign

Subject line: Schedule Meeting before you launch your next campaign.

Subject line: Reduce your costs with our solution!

Subject line: Schedule time to discuss how we can improve your next campaign

Here's the problem:

There's nothing in any of these subject lines that really benefits the buyer. Discussing how you can benefit the brand only benefits the salesperson. Wait, you say. Doesn't the promise of improving the next campaign constitute a benefit? NO! Think of the mindset of the person in charge of advertising. They don't come to work thinking "gee, I hope a total stranger with no direct knowledge of me, my company or my problems provides unsolicited advice which I can begin acting on right away." Instead, they're thinking: "this seller isn't in a position to know my unique needs (no matter how similar each customer's needs are, each and every one believes they are unique.)

So, what is the right subject line? It's the one that whets the reader's appetite, and does not immediately associate the seller with the thousands of other sellers who are using the same subject line.

For example, suppose we initially reach out to Chris's boss, Jean Smith the CMO. Jean tells us to contact Chris. Now our subject line is Jean Smith. Or, since we were going to tell Chris about our successful work with the XYZ brand, we use the subject line XYZ. Chris doesn't know you but will surely open an email that mentions their boss or their competition.

Unless the subject line relates to them, your email failed the subject line test.

> **The Takeaway: Your subject line, combined with the sender's email address, determines whether your email will be opened or not. Make sure one of them connect with the reader. What's in it for them, not you is the test question you need to apply when evaluating subject lines.**

Unlocking The 2nd Gate: The Opening Line

There is a world of difference between how to begin an email and how to begin a sales meeting. This line might work in an actual meeting, but fails as an opening line to an email:

"My name is ___ and I am the (title/function) with (company name) and I wanted to reach out to tell you ___."

This common email opening fails the opening line test. Why? Because it's 17 unnecessary words not counting the fill-in blanks. 17 words before this email sender finally got to their point.

My name is is not needed. I spotted who you were in your email address. I saw it again in your email signature along with your company name and your title.

I wanted to reach out to you is the writing equivalent of filler words such as "actually" or "basically" that nervous salespeople can't stop themselves from repeating when presenting.

You open the gate to the reader's attention span when you get to your point with the fewest words.

The less a person knows you the less interested they will be in reading your long emails, especially if they have a mountain of emails from people they do know. Your first sentence needs to deliver value or the reader will stop reading.

> *The Takeaway: The opening line determines if the reader will read the rest. That's true of books, blogs, articles and your emails. Assume the reader has only enough attention span for one sentence. Don't waste their time by telling them what they already know or don't need to know.*

The 3rd gate: The body of your email.

Sometimes the best way to keep this gate from locking is to leave it out entirely.

Let's look at a typical email — just the shape, not the words. You can tell without reading it that it looks like a mass-mailed email. You can tell it's not personalized; it looks like the kind of letter people delete as soon as they glance at it.

To:
From:
Re: XXXX **(Subject line)**

Dear XXX,
XXXXXXXXXXXXXXXXXXXXXXXXXXXXXXXXXXXXXXXXXXXXXXXXX
XXXXXXXXXXXXXXXXXXX
XXXXXXXXXX. **(Opening line)**

XXXXXXXXXXXXXXXXXXXXXXXXXXXXXXXXXXXXXXXXXXXXXXXX
XXXXXXXXXXXXXXXXXXXXXXXXXXXXXXXXXXXXXXXXXXXXXXXX
XXXXXXXXXXXXXXXXXXXXXXXXXXXXXXXXXXXXXXXXXXXXXXXX
XXXXXXXXXXXXXXXXX

Body

Hypertext links

XXXXX.

XXXXXXXXXXXXXXXXXXXXXXXXXXXXXXXXXXXXXXXXXXXXXXXX
XXXXXXXXXXXXXXXXXXXXXXXXXXXXXXXXXXXXXXXXXXXXXXXX
XXXXXXXXXXXXXXXXXXXXXXXXXXXXXXXXXXXXXXXXXXXXXXXX
XXXXXXXXXX XXXXXXX.

XXXXXXXXXXXXXXXXXXXXXXXXXXXXXXXXXXXXXXXXXXXXXXXX
XXX **(Call to Action)**

XXXX,
Name
Signature

What was this salesperson trying to communicate that required the body? There is no arguing that the subject line, opening line and CTA (call-to-action) are essential. But the body? And, if we don't know the person, can we really expect them to click on our links? Obviously, if all we wanted to ask for is a short phone appointment, this approach feels like we are circling that point rather than going directly there. And, if we are trying to impress this person with our personalized message — in our first email to them — this shape will lock the reader's attention in the off position.

> ***The Takeaway: Consider the risk of losing the reader
> when deciding whether or not to include an email
> body in a first email to that person.***

The 4th gate: the CTA (call-to-action)

The right CTA drives engagement. Are two CTAs better than one?

One of the oldest expressions in sales, which has been studied and proven true: if you give a person too many choices, they will make none. One of the newest expressions in the digital age: don't expect strangers to engage with your links or attachments.

Too many CTAs locks this important gate.

In the above example, the reader was given three choices: to click on either of two links in the body or to skip down to the final CTA in the last line above the signature. That's too many choices. Statistically, the user will most likely not take any action.

An exception would be if this email follows a conversation during which the customer specifically asked for link access to your content. Once you meet and they trust you, multiple links may be ok. But, if this is your first contact with a person who doesn't know you, simplify the CTA process by only offering one, easy-to-agree-to, safe-looking choice, like these calls-to-action:

- Please reply with an answer to a question (make sure it's a sincere question, and not a sales set-up like "wouldn't you agree that you could use some help...?")
- Please reply with a date/time to talk

For most salespeople, the purpose of the CTA is to do one of three things:

1. Learn if the person is interested in your service/product/content
2. Learn if the person is "qualified"
3. Learn when the person would be interested in talking

The Echo Seller, however, is looking to inform with content that inspires the other person (who we believe is in a position to influence) to share with their peers. We're not necessarily looking to qualify or meet them. Given that, consider not using any CTA when writing to people you want to educate but not qualify or meet.

> *The Takeaway: The purpose of the CTA is to create a step toward buying, but it makes the sender look more like a salesperson. Consider not using any CTA when you want the person to read (and possibly share) your email without the distraction of a sales pitch. And, if you chose to include a CTA, don't use more than one.*

Testing: Knowing versus Guessing

Quality emails and InMails take time to create. It can be painful to write, edit, re-write, show a friend who suggests big and small changes, starting from scratch and re-writing all over again. By the time you come up with one "great" email or InMail (or phone "script") you are exhausted. Coming up with two or three different "great" emails, InMails or phone scripts can feel overwhelming. For that reason, most sellers don't conduct A-B or A-B-C tests. Which is the biggest mistake they can make.

Recall our discussion from earlier in the book about the many psychological filters that fool us into thinking we know what the customer would like best. What looks exactly right for us, might look completely wrong to a customer.

Conventional sellers work-around this problem by using the quantity method: send out the same email template to enough people until one of them responds with the desired action.

But that won't work for the Echo Seller. We need quality — not the seller's view of quality but the customer's view. To hit that right, experiment with at least an A-B test, where you vary the time of day, day of the week, email length as well as the way you handle all four gates.

For example, we just talked about the risks and rewards for including one CTA. Why not test to see which CTA works best or whether leaving out any CTA works even better? Don't take my word for what works best for you and your unique territory. And, don't assume you already know how everyone thinks unless you determine that with testing.

Another advantage of testing is psychological. When you are focusing on creating different versions, you will feel empowered. If you go into the world with only one approach, unless you hit a bullseye the first time, you will conclude that Echo Selling doesn't work and you will revert back to your old way … which sadly puts you in competition with most of your peers who think the same way and write the same way.

Testing & Tracking: Measuring Quantity versus Quality

Echo Selling is a quality game, not a quantity game.

Measuring quality improvements requires constant testing and great tracking skills. The more motivated you are to test and track, the better you will get at both skills.

But most sellers I meet are weak in both skills. Why? Because they rely on their technology to do all the work for them.

To be clear, a robust CRM like SFdc (Salesforce.com) is great at counting things, assuming no inputting errors (of course, inputting errors are rampant, beginning with the "error" of not regularly updating data).

But quality is measured by comparing multiple data points, such as combining sales cycle with deal size with customer type with lead source to determine which word choice, marketing effort or sales strategy outperformed the others. To measure quality, you need to combine the right factors. Therefore, to measure quality, a custom report is needed. Even though most sellers have a CRM, few know how to create a custom report.

To understand the importance of this one technical skill, I will share a story about sharpening your axe. When motivational speakers use this story, they make the point that your skills (your axe) always need sharpening. But I will introduce a new ending for Echo Sellers.

Two woodcutters compete. The one on the right chops wood without stopping and thinks they will win because of their relentless effort. The one on the left keeps stopping to sharpen their axe, and (surprise!) they win. The lesson: both players used the same great tool. But only the winner knew how to properly use the tool. In sales, it's not the tool (technology). Everyone has access to the same tool set. And at least a dozen of them at any given moment are trying to get an appointment with your leads, prospects and customers. Given that, it's the human skills that will give you a competitive edge.

> *The Takeaway: Learn how to properly use your sales tools, especially when all of your competitors are also using those same tools.*

Be Your Own Cheerleader: Tracking Can Change Your Outlook

Whether or not you can properly track, do you know why you are tracking?

Most sellers are taught that tracking finds "what works." The problem with sales is that nothing works in the conventional sense of the word. If you are great, like a great baseball hitter, you mostly don't hit a homerun. No matter how good you are as a salesperson, the majority of emails will go unanswered, most calls are ignored, most first meetings don't result in a next step, most proposals don't close. If you become twice as good at closing as well as four times as good at producing great leads you will still mostly not close.

Psychologically, this can be depressing, especially for the new-to-sales professional who hasn't yet learned that you can still be successful even if you get more NOs than YESes.

The real benefit of tracking comes from looking at your numbers and finding at least one thing you can celebrate. The single most important lesson you learn from finding that win is that you made it happen with your efforts. Without that insight, everything looks like either good luck or bad luck. But, that one win is proof that in a world where a lot of things are outside your control, you control the outcome.

People often say they will believe it when they see it. Sorry, but that is wrong. You won't see it until you believe it.

> *The Takeaway: The first purpose of collecting data is to get you to change your beliefs. Once you do, you will see all kinds of things you can do to build on that momentum and create the world you want to live in.*

Be Your Own Coach: Change Yourself, Change Your Numbers

In my first sales job, every time my boss told me they wanted me to hit "better numbers" I pointed out that they were preaching to the choir. I, too, was in favor of those numbers improving. It wasn't me; it was the customer that wasn't playing along. They were the ones that weren't reacting properly to my prospecting, presenting and closing efforts. If only they would change, then my numbers would change.

Eventually I learned one of the most important life lessons: if my plans depend on other people changing, I will fail — unless I change first.

As I changed into an Echo Seller, I began to apply that to my sales numbers. And, when I did, I changed my numbers. Eventually, my numbers leveled off, which experts in numbers call Regression toward the Mean, which means your outlier results will revert back to "average results" over time.

Pop psychology says that we can avoid this if we create new habits and maintain them for 21 days. I spent most of my adult life hoping and praying for that to be the case, but I found it was only true for bad habits. For good habits in general and Echo Selling in particular, the only way to maintain ever-rising results is to keep changing.

Conventional sellers think they are doing everything right, which is why they seldom change either themselves or their results. Echo Sellers think differently. They see a constantly changing world. They aren't merely confident because they've been successful, their confidence comes from being able to keep up with constant change. They don't do things because they once worked; they keep changing in order to keep finding a new way to hit ever-rising goals. They maintain this changed state not because some invisible habit pulls them into place but because of a daily decision to get an increasing number of easy sales.

To get the results I have promised through Echo Selling, make a daily decision to practice Echo Selling. And, when you do, your numbers will keep changing in the right direction.

> *The Takeaway: Echo Selling is selling the right way. To realize the promised success, you need to make a daily decision to experience ongoing improvement.*

Putting It All Together: Put One Foot in Front of The Other (And Alternate Feet)

I wrote this book with this moment in mind.

I highly recommend you read the whole book again and do all the exercises.

Here are five steps to get most of the benefit if you don't have enough time to re-read the whole thing:

1. Just read The Takeaway parts — I created them as your study notes.

2. If you don't have the time to complete all the exercises described in Part 3 — (**Echo Selling Word Choice and Performance Tips**), work on your answer to What Makes You Different.

3. Create your InMail, email and phone scripts — if there's no time to develop more than one version (A — B test), begin with one. You can always tweak the wording on a second attempt.

4. Consider your target list - I recommended you begin with at least three targets but if you are short on time, just pick one.

5. The key to making Echo Selling work is the same key for all worthwhile goals: give yourself a due date to begin.

Final Thoughts

My best ideas are ones that I learned from my clients and tried in my own sales. When those things work for me, I pass them on. I wrote Echo Selling after closing sales using the tactics and strategies I described. I believe they will also work for you—and I want to hear from you when they do. Please reach out and share your success stories with me. Some of them might make their way into one of my workshops.

About the Author

Steve has trained more than 50,000 people in 5,000 in-person workshops, 500 sales kickoffs and hundreds of keynote speeches throughout North and South America, Europe, Asia and the Middle East. He has developed customized training for every sales role, client size and go-to-market strategy.

Steve's digital training includes virtual workshops, videos, online programs and podcasts. His clients range from global market leaders to start-ups across many industry verticals, with an emphasis in Advertising, Marketing, Finance, Media and Technology.

Clients rely on Steve to bring them the newest best-practice tactics and strategies he's observed around the world and to deliver his insights with passion and humor. Participants report a dramatic increase in confidence and a measurable improvement in performance.

Steve's latest book, Echo Selling, introduces salespeople to the influence of psychology, digital media and word-of-mouth on buying decisions and the new ways sellers must now train for success.

Sellers in every marketplace are experiencing challenges because of altered buying behaviors, which has caused the creation of specialized roles and the need for new skills. Steve's training has evolved to help sellers meet these demands with personalized coaching, unique workshops, fresh approaches to virtual delivery and a growing library of on-demand training programs, relevant to everyone from new hires to seasoned sales professionals.

CPSIA information can be obtained
at www.ICGtesting.com
Printed in the USA
BVHW051242040322
630605BV00005B/19